Pathfinder

Karen E. Channey
Donald D. Shaw

Published by:
The Athletic Institute
200 Castlewood Street
North Palm Beach, Fla.
U. S. A.

FIRST EDITION

Library of Congress Catalog Card Number 80-66466
ISBN 0-87670-060-1

Acknowledgements

"We express appreciation to Lynda Lyman Bassett for the Illustrations in this guide and to the United States Department of the Interior, Heritage Conservation and Recreation Service, Washington, D.C. 20240, for the Directory of Sources of Trails Information."

The Authors

Contents

PATHFINDER

List of Figures

Introduction

"Climb the mountains and get their good tidings;
Nature's peace will flow into you as sunshine into flowers;
The winds will blow their freshness into you and the storms
   their energy,
And cares will drop off like Autumn leaves."

John Muir (1838-1914)

YOUR LAND, OUR LAND

As this bountiful land of North America developed, the conflict soon became apparent between man's material desire to abuse the land and his spiritual need to enjoy the beautiful wilderness. As civilization expanded across the land from east to west and cities and towns began to emerge as shipping, business and manufacturing centers, this great pioneer society carved the first intrusion into the woodlands of America. The wild, wild west, as it has often been called, was a country to be feared and yet challenged. To begin with, it was a victory each time a settler claimed another tract of land, felled the forest, and began to cultivate a farm or pasture. The Homestead Act brought about the potential for desiring land owners to claim a section of ground, fence it, put on a cabin, tame it through cultivation and then claim it for their own. From the very beginning, there were people who could not tolerate the vast changes

9

and encroachments in the wilderness which were happening in our nation. These early explorers and trappers began hinting that there should remain an area where man could stretch his wings, and that being out in the wilderness alone or with a small group was part of the therapy and motivation that moved man throughout this great exploratory period. These early backpackers realized that this preservationary effort represented a kind of innocence that could help counter the evils that were being generated by the greed of an advancing civilization. Fortunately, there were a few loud voices heard from this group which caused Congress to grudgingly grant a concession for the establishment of a piecemeal wilderness heritage. Shortly after the turn of the century, they set aside a few remote tracts of land as primitive areas where nature could be left in peace. However, they did not restrict man from going on to that land if gold or coal was discovered. Then the wilderness areas had to give way to what they called "progress." Ranchers were given permission to graze cattle or sheep on the reserves, and mining and rock claims were allowed to be established which brought about roads and people infringing and encroaching upon even this small wilderness area. Through isolated efforts by the middle of the century, Congress had granted a more or less protected status to nearly 11 million acres of wilderness. Much of this legislation was in response to a growing group of people who recognized the necessity to preserve the land, and who later were to be called environmentalists.

With the passing of the wilderness Act in 1964, Congress attempted to consolidate these scattered primitive, roadless areas under a reasonable uniform policy. This act was designed to provide a guideline for the future management of a wilderness heritage that was obviously becoming more and more valuable with each passing day. Although it left a great deal to be desired, this act was a big step toward preserving some of America's finest back country. However, this act did not deter open and strip mining, cattle and sheep grazing, and did not essentially restrict petroleum exploration.

Even though a few halting steps have been taken to protect America's wilderness, we are still faced with the major problem today of preserving and protecting our nation's land, water, and wildlife resources. It has become increasingly apparent that we have permitted great rivers and lakes to become polluted by industrial and human waste, forests to be ruthlessly raized by lumbering interests, and wildlife to be ravaged by uncontrolled hunting. Chemical poisons are threatening wildlife breeding and feeding grounds. Ultimately, as a consequence of this ruthless destruction of our environment, man has himself become a threatened species. Greater and greater demands are placed upon our natural resources bank. Open space has been shrinking at an unprecedented rate. A million acres or more are lost each year to development for residential or commercial uses. In California alone, 375 acres a day amounting to 145,000 acres a year of agricultural land is turned to urban uses. Of the original 127 million acres of wetlands and marshlands in the United States, crucial to many forms of wildlife, over 45 million have been destroyed by draining, filling, and dredging. In many cases, powerful commercial interests have resisted the establishment of new federal and state parks. Typically, the battle to develop Redwood National Park in California has been fought by spokesmen for the redwood lumber industry. They claimed that the National Park Services plan to preserve the giant redwoods along the state's northern coast was "unnecessary, confiscatory, and economically depressing and would threaten employment in the area." Today, 85 percent of the original redwood forests have been logged. Only 2.5 percent is protected in state parks.

Present policy calls for potential recreation wilderness sites to be studied and the proposals aired to the public. President Carter is suggesting additional wilderness lands be designated in various states, particularly throughout the western United States and Alaska. However, the present crunch on energy indicates that these proposals will have a rough road ahead. As the shortage of oil and oil products becomes more evident each day, shifting to other energy sources such as coal will be emphasized and many wilderness areas will be jeopardized in the interest of the national energy policy. After all sides have had their say, the future of our priceless wilderness will be settled by compromise, and tragically, it is the backpacker and his concerns that will most probably end up being only a "voice crying in the wilderness." We estimate that it will take at least twice as much land as we now have to accommodate the numbers that will look to the beauty and solitude of the wilderness as a respite from urban, slum, and pollution by the end of this century. With no immediate relief in sight for years, it then becomes necessary for the people to enjoy the peace and beauty of the back country, and to understand that we have to bear the brunt of keeping what we have intact, clean, and usable. We must no longer treat the wilderness when we go into it as a consumable commodity. Those of us who have visited a "popular" campsite can recall the scattered refuse, sour pits, the landscape and trees hacked up for firewood, and all of the fragile ground cover has disappeared by compression of many people into a restricted area. Simply stated, the problem is one of balance. No longer can we afford the luxury of the in-discriminate campfire or cooking fire at every camp. The beauty and charm of a flickering campfire flame that begins at dusk and goes on into the night cannot be denied. However, with the influx of many campers and backpackers, we can now no longer provide the resources to support this beauty. There simply isn't enough fuel left around our campsites in the wilderness to continue to make a campfire practical. Possible exceptions are along rivers and streams where an annual supply of firewood is brought down by the spring runoff. Even when you're so fortunate as to find this condition available, keep your fire no larger than is ab-solutely necessary. Fuel the fire with small pieces of wood that can be removed from a lonely wood shoreline or log jam without destroying the character of the land. The fire pit should be completely erased before you leave so that there is no visible sign that you had a fire at camp. A fire should never be considered unless a permit has been secured in advance. When conditions are favorable for a campfire, the camp should be sited on open sand or dirt, rock, or other exposed surfaces. Leave the lush meadow and the alpine morraine in their original state, as the effect of an overnight stay on these delicate areas will take years to overcome. Your skill in choosing a campsite and your attitude toward a campfire will make a great contribution to the future of the back country. We need to learn to live with the forest, passing through it without leaving a mark. Its future depends in large part on what we don't leave as we pass through it. It has often been said that we should leave only our footprints, taking nothing away but memories. To pass through and to enjoy its beauty should be considered a non-consumable resource. So we recommend that you go into the forest, back country and wilderness, visit your favorite areas, enjoy them thoroughly, but leave them just the way you found them. Unfortunately, the time will undoubtedly come when it will be necessary to restrict the number of people who can enter the wilderness at a given time, and in some cases, closing areas completely until nature has had a chance to heal her wounds. The diligence you exercise in your own backpacking adventures will help decide when these restrictions must come.

IMPACT OR IMPRINT

All living things, including man are meshed in an interdependent web of life. Even the most subtle change has far reaching effects. Overcrowding will be the biggest problem facing the American wilderness even though at this time most of it has virtually never been touched. One of the basic factors that determines the ultimate impact people have on an area is how far they have to travel to get to it. Degradation and damage in the wilderness is generally proportional to the number of miles a place is from the trail head. It's natural for hikers to seek out flats alongside of a lake, places where smaller streams cross a trail, or those areas that offer spectacular views. Most backpackers as they move along the trail are looking for campsites nearest water supplies. It seems that the trail itself is an outward sign of security to them. Therefore, unfortunately, many camps are located within a few feet of the trail and close to available water. With an extra effort, choose a campsite that is at least two to three hundred yards from the trail. Just a few minutes will put you into virgin territory away from the hacked landscape, the cast-off junk, and the badly worn campsite. Go a little further up and down the creek and you'll be rewarded with a delightful spot to pitch your tent, have a nearby source of water, and also the most choice thing of all, peace and quiet. It should be obvious that by going farther into the wilderness we will reduce the over-crowding and damage that occurs.

A longer trip leads you into the heart of the beautiful parks and back country where you can spend a few days in the serenity and silence of the deep forest. It means giving up more frequent weekend trips, but it also means protecting our fragile wonderland of the back country.

Surely, American's founding fathers took pride in viewing the immensity of the land around them and thought "how bountiful." Indeed it was, for as far as the eye could see there were rambling meadows, forested hills, wild rivers, glorious mountains and valleys, and a seemingly endless land. As generations of Americans have lived and died, they have passed along the heritage of rich lands and waters. With that heritage, however, was passed an inherent attitude that the resources of this great nation were limitless. Traditionally, Americans have viewed their nation as long on land and short on cash. In the name of technology and progress, we've harnessed our wild rivers, ripped up the soils to reach deep mineral deposits, and cleared the forested hills with a commercial axe and saw for timber. Throughout the ages, we have become great in a material sense through the use of our natural resources. Demands upon our resources grew as the nation witnessed the press of a rising population that needed homes to live in, food to eat, clothing to wear, convenience for ease of lifestyle, and myriads of other products and services. Today, the people press continues.

In 1979, there were approximately 220 million people in America. By the year 2020, almost 300 million are expected to populate the land of this nation. With those added numbers comes the questions: Where will they live? How will we feed them? What resources will provide the vast quantities of energy needed to produce goods and provide the services required by the increasing millions. Seemingly then, there will be an ever-increasing demand upon our resources and surely exhaustion of some of them is not beyond comprehension. We were inconvenienced by the energy crisis during the winter of '73 and '74 and now again during the summer of '79. The experts now portend a serious metal crisis in the not-too-distant future, and a world-wide food crisis has been predicted. This kind of doomsday philosophy of the nation's complete exhaustion of resources and eventual elimination of life support systems is perhaps too extreme. Intelligence and ingenuity ascribed to the American people are not without justification. We are awakening to the need for more judicious use of the country's natural resources, and the conservation or environmental movement is gaining support each day.

We need to have concern for proper land use planning. Wise use of our remaining lands and waters is necessary so that we have sufficient in the future to feed and house new people and provide them with necessities, as well as to give all Americans the opportunity to enjoy the amenities of the wilderness. Professionals in the field believe that the protection of natural open space is not just a matter of providing a decorative backdrop to everyday life. Rather, it is the very source of existence. We must foster intelligent use of lands and waters, and act now to set aside and protect both environmentally and recreationally these significant resources.

Each of us as backpackers should work toward these goals. Not only must we strive for ultimate land and water preservation, but also the users of our present wilderness areas should be educated and conduct themselves with good manners following an ethical code such as the following that should be accepted and used by all backpackers.

I will:

1. Not hike alone and will register with the proper forest or resource headquarters before entering the wilderness to avoid causing unnecessary anxiety and search and rescue mission.

2. Keep to designated trails and camp and designated campgrounds obeying all resource management regulations.

3. Not harm or damage or frighten if I can avoid it any living thing, plant or animal. Neither will I disturb rocks or fallen trees or stream beds unnecessarily.

4. Bury all biodegradable waste restoring the ground cover as much as possible. Non-biodegradable waste such as plastic containers and aluminum cans I will carry out as I carried them in.

5. Bring no unseemly noise to compete with the music of the water and the winds and the voices of the wilderness.

6. Build campfires only where it is permitted and gather only such dead wood as is absolutely necessary. I prefer packing in the wilderness stove and leaving fallen wood where it lies.

7. In short, I'll respect the wilderness and its ways and leave it untrampled so that the visitor who follows me will experience "the tonic of wildness" even as I have experienced it.

MAKING IT ALL COUNT

One of the most inspiring and self-satisfying activities that modern man has embraced in his efforts to escape from the fetters and pressures of civilization has been the adventurous sport of backpacking. The term "backpacking" usually refers to an extended camping trip into the wilderness taken by an individual who uses only his feet for transportation, and his back to carry all necessary supplies. This type of travel was not unknown to the early pioneer or mountainman, but has since grown dramatically in its widespread popularity as a form of recreational expression. This is primarily due to the increased comfort and efficiency available through modern equipment, as well as to the fairly recent discovery of the healing powers and uplifting effects with which this activity tends mens souls.

There are several unique benefits which make backpacking available and appealing to almost everyone.

1 — It provides a means to the enjoyment of any type of terrain (mountain, desert, seashore or forest) year

around, and there are numerous places to go near most any locality.

2 — It opens the door to beautiful scenery that would not have been accessible in any other way, and is a fairly inexpensive means for the average income person to experience a vacation in the "Great outdoors."

3 — It is an enjoyable form of exercise, helping to maintain strong muscles and lungs and overall good health.

4 — It is a psychologically and spiritually fulfilling way to strengthen self-esteem, experience a relaxing change from the daily routine, and to achieve harmony with self and nature as one returns to an appreciation of "simple" things.

5 — It offers the choice of either going alone and increasing independence, individuality, and personal solitude and quiet, or of going with friends or family, and through the informal setting building relationships, molding character, developing group or family unity and teamwork, and laying the foundation for fun, and cherished memories.

6 — Packing may also be combined with many other outdoor activities, such as mountain climbing, skiing, snowshoeing, fishing, bird watching, rockhounding, spelunking, and many others.

Whether you plan to hike the Appalachian, Finger Lake, or Pacific Crest Trails, or are just planning an overnight trip into the local canyon, desert, or beach, there is a certain amount of knowledge and skill which you will first need before starting off. The purpose of this book is to provide both the essential information necessary for a fun, successful backpacking experience, as well as to help the people involved in most forms of outdoor travel adventure to avoid doing anything which would be harmful to the environmental quality of the land. Our wilderness areas are best preserved by simultaneously exposing people to their beauties and teaching them not to be destructive to their delicately balanced life-forces. Therefore, we are encouraging the current change in outdoor philosophy from the old pioneer camping ethic of "use the land to make man comfortable" to the more responsible wilderness camping ethic of "leave no trace."

So let's begin with the first and probably most important phase of backpacking — the planning process.

1 Trip Preparation

PLANNING THE TRIP

Part of the fun of any outing is the planning stage. As you and your friends decide where to go, when you can get away, and what equipment you'll need to make it all work, you can begin to really experience that feeling of freedom that comes from backpacking. To maximize the experience the outing should extend over a week or more. During this time, the wilderness experience takes on a whole new dimension. As the days pass, you begin to see things more clearly, to notice delicate beauty and intricate relationships you probably haven't been aware of before. This change doesn't occur overnight. It takes place slowly in attitudes and actions over a period of several days. To know this special feeling for the first time you must spend several days in the back country. Heading out on a long back-packing trip is probably the best way to introduce yourself to the pleasures of the trail, but it's not something to take lightly. Back country makes certain demands on you and you must be prepared to meet them. Therefore, this requires a trip plan. This plan might be nothing more than a rough menu for a short outing or it might be a complex series of check lists for a month on the trail. In either case, the plan will have a significant impact on the success of your journey.

Every good plan considers four separate but highly related stages, each depending somewhat on the others.

They include the **time table, equipment selection, food and cooking gear,** and **safety planning**. We should also say that it's foolish to attempt any hike alone, especially a long one. It's pretty dangerous for even a qualified outdoorsman to be alone when he is walking on the trail and sprains an ankle or has a bad fall. Also, even the planning is more fun when it's done together and you're able to enjoy the unique contributions of each person in your backpacking group.

Long-range planning includes getting yourself in good physical condition and acquiring the necessary (and when possible) first-class equipment. You can get in shape by first taking short walks and then working up to full weekend hikes with a full pack. However, if you haven't been regularly exercising, you may need to consult with your doctor and be especially careful and take it easy the first few days. The key words to remember here are "thoroughly plan and be alert," as you first get ready during the planning stages and then are observant throughout the entire course of an outing.

These are the general steps which will help you to "be prepared" and have a successful and enjoyable experience.

1 — Set a date at least one month ahead. For an outing of more than a few days, try not to travel alone, but if you must, stick to frequently used trails in case you become sick or injured. When choosing group companions, consider their attitude, strength and ability, equipment, and experience. Also, consider the time of year and weather reports. All of these factors can affect the degree of enjoyment of a trip.

2 — When selecting the type of trail, time schedule, and overall length of the trip, keep in mind the hiking capability of each person involved. This is especially necessary when any children are part of the group. Allow ample time for an unhurried trip and consider the present as well as the future predicted weather conditions. Each wilderness area requires different planning, equipment, clothing, and energy due to the change in environmental and climatic conditions involved (which also effect group morale and safety). Select the desired route or trail and get all appropriate and current topographical maps for that particular location. Know where the local ranger stations are, inquire from recent visitors about the trail, and check with

local land management officials (Game Department, Forest Service, etc.) for present conditions and the current rules and regulations which you will be expected to follow.

3 — Always make a preliminary checklist of necessary items. If you are going with a group (preferably a minimum of four people or a maximum of twenty-five for wilderness travel), choose a person or persons (at least a leader and assistant) to organize the trip and see that all common items (shovel, rope, etc.) are not duplicated and are equally distributed among all members. Also, delegate to each person in the group or family their specific area of responsibility (such as food, utensils, sleeping shelter, etc.).

4 — All people in the group need to be familiar with final plans for take-off time, expected length of travel, and selected camping spots for each day in case separation from the leader of the entire group occurs.

5 — Pack as much as possible ahead of time. Some things may even be packed a week or more in advance. However, don't buy perishables too early and prevent foods from contaminating each other by separate packaging. Prepare as much food as possible at home. (See Cooking and Food Section). Pack as little gear as possible and include many multi-purpose items.

6 — Always inspect all equipment and make a last minute double check of your list before leaving. Try out any new equipment or trial foods at home or on short trips before taking them on longer outings. Be aware of new developments in food and equipment and don't be afraid to experiment **before** the trip.

7 — Sign all trail registers so you can easily be located. Leave travel schedule in writing with family, friends, or civil authorities. Include who is going, where trailhead is located, what route you are using, equipment carried, type of vehicle used for transportation (model, color, license), estimated time of return (plan for any probable delays), and list any limitations of group members (allergies, handicaps, etc.). Make sure you have trail

camping and fire permits (or wilderness permits) where needed. Sign out with local authorities and leave a time schedule in the front car window.

8 — Eat a good balanced meal the night before leaving and get eight hours of good quality sleep. Breakfast should consist of light sugary foods which are small and easily digested to prevent stomach upsets on the trail.

9 — Upon return from the trip, store all equipment in one special place (most of it can fit in your pack) and make all necessary repairs **before** putting away. Air out all sleeping bags, wash the clothes and cooking equipment, and make any needed changes in your checklist for the next trip.

These general steps suggested in the planning process need to be followed. However, there are many other concerns that will affect the backpacker that require individual skills. We now offer you that information beginning with the map and compass in Chapter 3.

2 Map & Compass

Any backpacker who's felt the embarrassment of having to stop at a home or cottage and ask directions to find his way, has immediately recognized the need to know how to use a map and compass. Even more disconcerting is the backpacker lost in the wilderness who either does not have a map or compass or does not know how to use them if they are at hand. Although the backpacker is sometimes like the Indian brave who said, "Me not lost, teepee lost", indicating generally that he does have a potential for self survival, still desires and almost requires a practical choice of routes to get from one place to another. The good backpacker should know how to find his way through any kind of terrain. Whether you are hiking through forests or mountains, across deserts or plains, your best friend will be your compass and map. It can tell you where you are and how to get where you want to go.

MAPS, THE ILLUSTRATED EARTH

Knowing how to read a map is a great first step toward expanding your horizons in backpacking, letting you know what to expect of the country, and allowing you to follow the trails wherever they might lead. (See Fig. 2.0)

If you intend to leave the roads and trails to explore the wilderness, you'll have to know accurately where you are headed and how to get back. Knowing how to use a map and compass will give you this added dimension. The best maps

SWALLOW CANYON QUADRANGLE
UTAH-COLORADO
7.5 MINUTE SERIES (TOPOGRAPHIC)

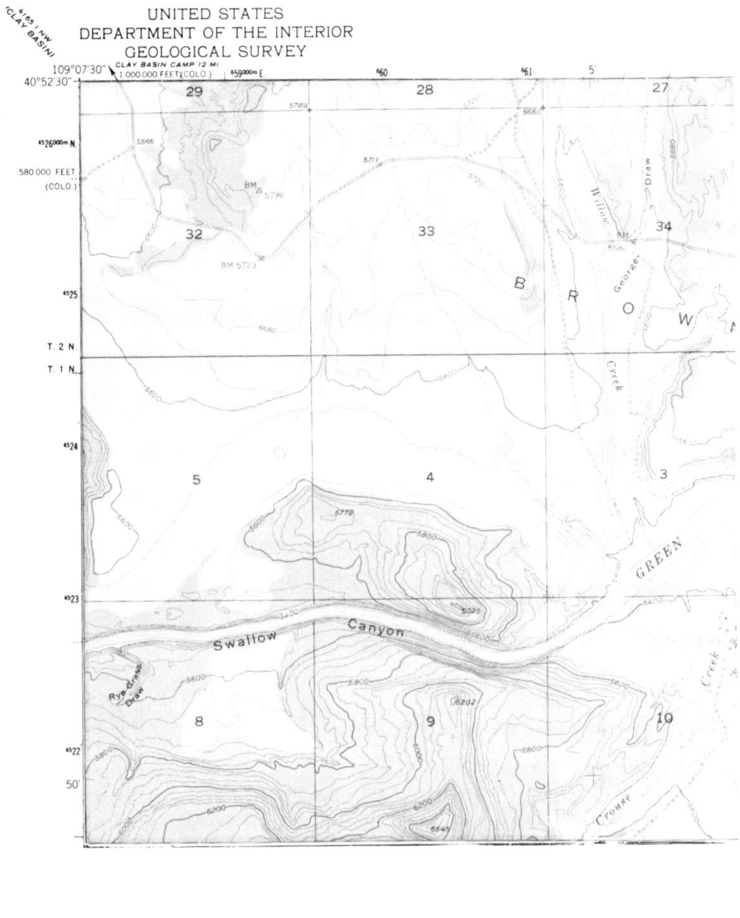

Fig. 2.0 Cut of topographical map.

for hiking are topographic. To get such a map, send a postcard to Map Information Office, U.S. Geological Survey, General Services Building, 18th and F Streets, N.W., Washington, D.C. 20405, requesting a free, topographical map index circular of the state you expect to hike in and a free folder describing topographic mpas. The index circular has a small map of the state divided into sections or quadrangles. For each quadrangle, there is a separate map. Find out which quadrangle you plan to backpack in, the order that map. You often have a choice of the 7.5-minute or the 15-minute maps for the specific area. The 15-minute map covers four times the area and as a result are less detailed. When ordering the map, name the quadrangle, include a money order or check for the proper amount. If you are ordering a map that is east of the Mississippi River, send to the Geological Survey in Weashington. For areas west of the River, send to the U.S. Geological Survey, Federal Center, Denver, Colorado 80200. You might also find that maps of your locality are sold in sporting goods stores, city and county buildings, or other locations close to you.

MAP READING AND CONTOURS

For the beginning backpacker, the first skill to be learned is how to read the map correctly. Terrain details are shown on a topographic map by means of map symbols. (See Figs. 2.1 & 2.2) There are several types which are often printed in "colors" for quicker reading. Those items that are printed in black are the work of man: roads, railroads, cities, bridges, boundaries, names, etc. A good well-traveled road is shown with two solid lines; a poor road by two broken lines, and a path with a single broken line. On some maps, improved highways are shown in red. A railroad is one or more lines with many cross lines suggesting the typical railroad tracks. Black rectangles or squares are buildings and a rectangle topped by a cross shows a church or if topped by a flag represents a schoolhouse. The color blue indicates water. A blue line is generally a brook, a blue band is a river, and a large blue blotch is a pond or lake. Contour lines showing height and depth of hills and valleys are indicated by brown lines. Every point on one has the same altitude and if you follow a heavy brown line on a map you'll

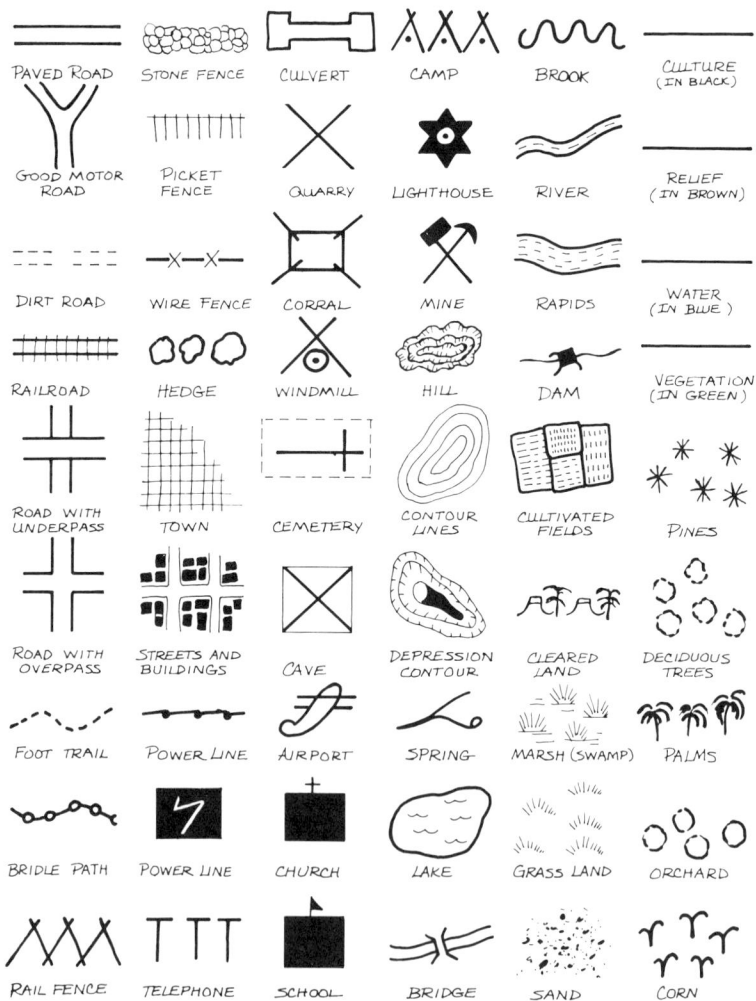

PAVED ROAD	STONE FENCE	CULVERT	CAMP	BROOK	CULTURE (IN BLACK)
GOOD MOTOR ROAD	PICKET FENCE	QUARRY	LIGHTHOUSE	RIVER	RELIEF (IN BROWN)
DIRT ROAD	WIRE FENCE	CORRAL	MINE	RAPIDS	WATER (IN BLUE)
RAILROAD	HEDGE	WINDMILL	HILL	DAM	VEGETATION (IN GREEN)
ROAD WITH UNDERPASS	TOWN	CEMETERY	CONTOUR LINES	CULTIVATED FIELDS	PINES
ROAD WITH OVERPASS	STREETS AND BUILDINGS	CAVE	DEPRESSION CONTOUR	CLEARED LAND	DECIDUOUS TREES
FOOT TRAIL	POWER LINE	AIRPORT	SPRING	MARSH (SWAMP)	PALMS
BRIDLE PATH	POWER LINE	CHURCH	LAKE	GRASS LAND	ORCHARD
RAIL FENCE	TELEPHONE	SCHOOL	BRIDGE	SAND	CORN

Fig. 2.1 Common map symbols

26

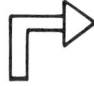

STRAIGHT AHEAD

TURN RIGHT

TURN LEFT

ROCKS

DANGER OR
MESSAGE LEFT

GRASS

BRUSH

Fig. 2.2 Common trail signs

find a number. For instance consider a line by the number 150. Everything on that line lies 150 feet above sea level. The distance or interval of height between lines is stated on the map. This is usually 20 feet. Where lines are far apart, it means the ground slopes gently and may be a good campsite. Where they are close together, the hill is steep and hiking will be tough. Where lines are highly crowded indicates a sharp drop-off or a cliff. The top of a prominent hill may be indicated by a number which gives the altitude or crest of the hill. Woodland areas are sometimes printed in green. This is often useful to the backpacker, so when ordering your map, specify "woodland copy." Whether across country is but a few hundred yards or many miles, the backpacker needs to know how far he has to travel to his destination or how far away a certain landmark is. The experienced backpacker under normal circumstances wouldn't attempt a trip unless he knew as fully as possible the distance between him and his goal. Perhaps the greatest numer of all rescue attempts have had to be launched for someone who tried a shortcut across land he didn't know with a map he couldn't read. The scales at the bottom of a map afford several ways to measure or determine distance. (1) A ratio 1 to 24,000 or 1 to 62,500; (2) a scale divided into miles and fractions; (3) a scale in thousands of feet; and (4) a metric scale. On a map in the scale of 1 to 24,000, one inch on the map represents 2,000 feet in the field. Even simpler are maps in the scale 1 to 62,500 where the number of inches of the map gives you roughly the number of miles on the ground. To know how far you have to travel or how far away a landmark is, simply measure the distance on the map, take a piece of paper and mark on its edge the distance between the two points of your route on the map. Then check this with the scale at the bottom of the map and read off the distance or copy the scale from the map along the edge of the paper and use the paper for measuring. If you plan to cover an area extensively, the 15-minute series map at a scale of 1 to 62,500 would be more useful to you. You can get a rough estimate of how far it is from one point on the map to another by using the width of your thumb. Place your thumb on the map so that from the starting point to the ending point, you determine how many thumb widths there are from one point to the next. Two thumb widths is generally about 6/10 of a mile. In average terrain, it takes about twelve minutes to walk 6/10 of a mile.

Maps are generally made using the following scales:

1:250,000	1 quarter inch = 1 mile	U.S. Series
1:125,000	½ inch = 1 mile	30-minute Series
1:62,500	1 inch = 1 mile	15-minute Series
1:24,000	2½ inches = 1 mile	7.5-minute Series

The series most often used is the 7.5 minute map of 1:24,000. It covers an area of 7½ minutes or a longitude of approximately 7½ miles wide.

Contour lines indicate the elevation above sea level. You may find contour lines a bit confusing at the beginning, but you'll soon be able to determine hills and mountains in terms of contour lines. If you'll note where the lines converge in a V, the point of this converging points up valleys and down ridges. Contour lines can be used as references to recognize a steep hill or a cliff by the close lines and the lines of a gentle slope by lines which are far apart. The topographical map quickly shows how steep the trails are, where the good water sources lie, and what areas are best suited for overnight stops along the way. (See Fig. 2.3) As you study the relative difficulty of each stretch of trail, you can more accurately decide how much time to allow for that particular bit of walking. This way you won't find yourself running out of energy just as you start up a grueling series of switchbacks still several hours from your intended destination. Carefully study the map prior to going on the backpacking trip. Note the trail conditions you can expect to encounter and plan each stage of your trip accordingly. When you are moving through steep alpine country or land that is edged by deep canyons, the topographic map will show where the best campsites may be found, where you can find a relatively flat spot with a convenient source of water instead of having to camp on a dry, steep hillside. The topographic map is essential to the cross country backpacker. Not only will it allow him to choose the path of least resistance and maximum enjoyment, it will allow him to take advantage of man-made features that work to his benefit. If the route crosses raging rivers, the map will show pipeline crossings, powerline access, or other features that will help him over the hazard. In a pure wilderness, the contours will show those places the water course is reasonably level

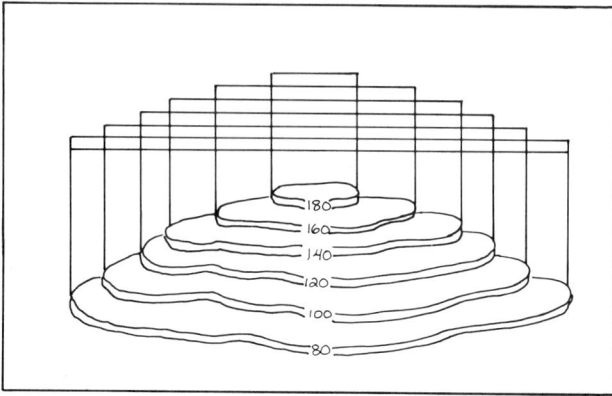

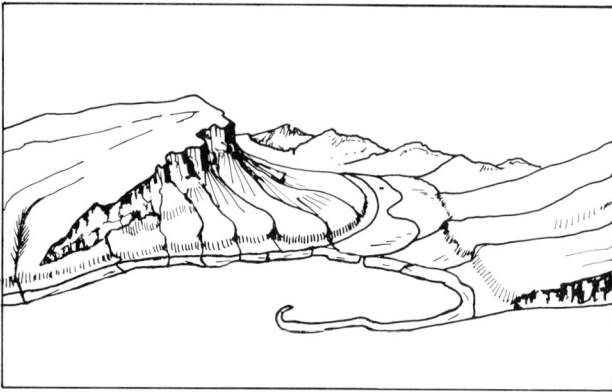

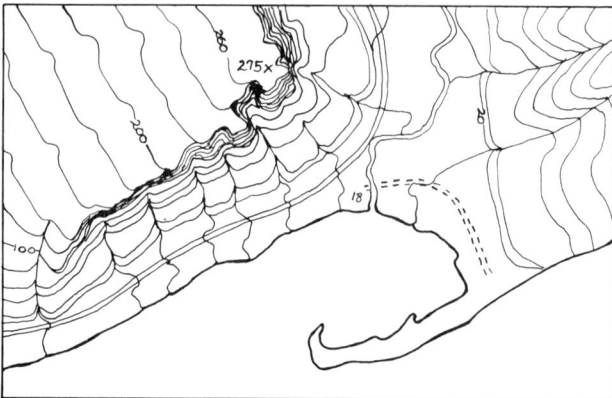

Fig. 2.3 Contour lines and landscape perspectives

affording at least a possible place to wade across. Conversely, the map will also show impassable cliffs and canyons that call for long detours. The actual elevations of most trails are noted on the topographic map. Another key planning tool — if the trail goes over a 6,000 foot pass and you are hiking in early summer, you might have to plan for walking certain stretches in the snow. In actual fact, the contour map can give you a complete preview of your trip, generally dictating the special equipment and techniques you need to enjoy it completely.

THE QUIVERING NEEDLE

Knowing how to read a map is obviously the first step towards finding correct directions while in the field and letting you know what to expect of the terrain you will be travelling in. If however, you intend to leave the roads and pathways to explore the wilderness as a backpacker, you'll have to know accurately how to get back. A compass gives you this ability. Almost everyone understands that a compass needle is supposed to point north, but it doesn't. The needle is magnetized and aligns itself with the magnetic field of the earth. In doing so, it points to what is called magnetic north. There are two popular ways of determining and recording the directions shown on a compass. One system uses four 90 degree quadrants for recording direction while the others use a 360 degree circle. Of these two, the latter is considerably easier to use and is the one most favored by the backpacker. The so-called "quadrant" system is almost exclusively reserved for survey and mapping use. A brief comparison of the two systems will show you the ease of using the "Azimuth" type of compass. The Azimuth system is found on virtually all popular brands of compasses for the non-professional. The backpacker has a choice of several suitable compasses and nearly all the desirable models are made by the same company — SILVA. The "SILVA" compass is also a device for measuring angles or finding a bearing so that this instrument fulfills the two basic orienteering needs of the backpacker. (See Fig. 2.4) It can find the correct direction from the map and it can point it out on the ground. The protractor type compass recommended for the novice backpacker is the Type 1 Silva model.

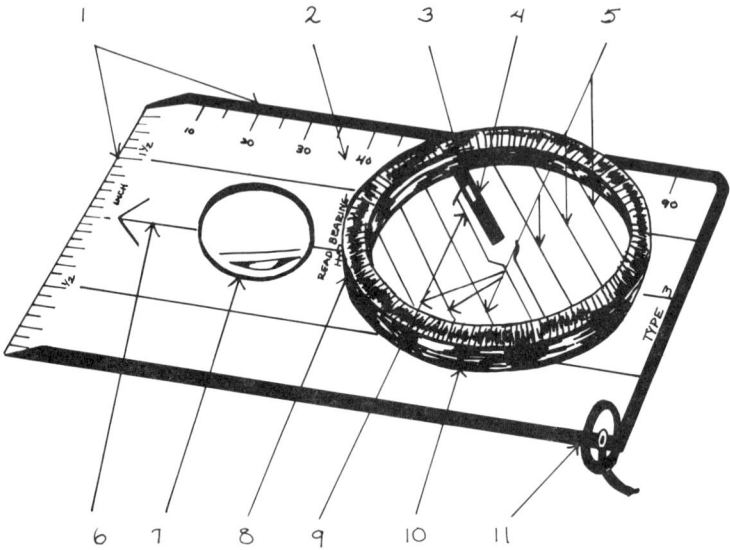

Fig. 2.4 The Parts of a 'Silva' Type 3 Compass

It's a well made instrument that will satisfy your needs. However, if you require greater refinement, Silva Type 3 or Type 4 models in which the needles are suspended in a liquid-filled housing will give you a quicker and more accurate reading.

A bearing is a horizontal angle fixing a point in respect to north. It is measured in a clockwise direction from north in degrees. There are 360 degrees in a full circle.

An early complication for most backpackers is the existence of three norths. **True north** is the actual direction of the north pole and can be ignored for all practical purposes for the backpacker. **Grid north** is the direction in which all the vertical grid lines point on a topographical map. **Magnetic north** is the direction toward which the magnetic needle points, that is, the magnetic north pole. The difference between magnetic north where the compass points and true north, the north pole, is called "declination". (See Fig. 2.5) On the bottom of a map you'll find a compass rose which will tell you how great the declination is. The line with the star at the end points to true north. The line with one-half arrow at the end shows which way the compass

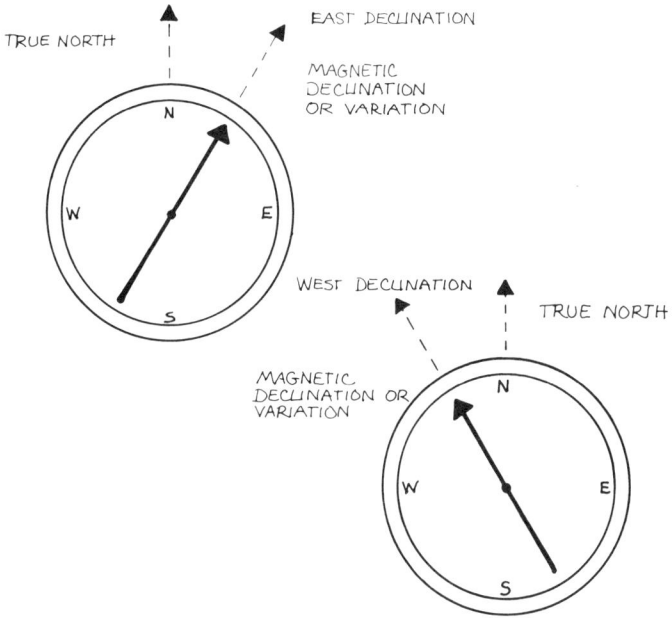

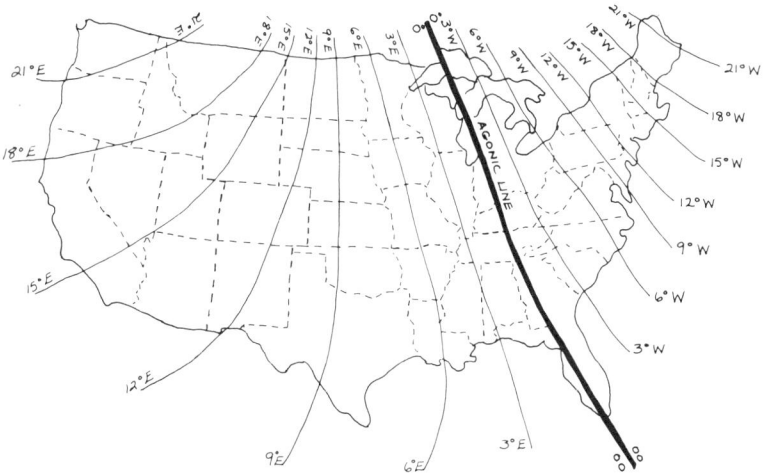

Fig. 2.5 East and west declination

needle will point to magnetic north and will also tell how many degrees away from true north. To find true north on the compass, let the needle point to the direction indicated on the map declination. The zero and N on the compass will then point true north. To allow for compass error (declination) when you are either following a given heading from a map or when locating the position of some observed landscape feature on the map you should: (1) find the correct degree and direction of variation or declination. If the declination is westerly, the needle is pulled left or north on your compass; if the declination is easterly, turn the compass so the needle is to the right (east of north). Be sure to maintain the correct variation while reading the Azimuth or citing an object; (2) turn the direction arrow of the compass to the given bearing or object cited. Then slide over the arrow to find a landmark to follow or if identifying an object read off the true bearing on the Azimuth ring. Around the ouside of the compass are markings divided into 360 degrees. (See Fig. 2.6) They will read counter-clockwise. North is always 0 degrees (360 degrees on a compass), south is always 180 degrees, east is 90 degrees and west is 270 degrees. To find out which direction is being cited hold the compass level and line it on a true north-south setting (remember the declination). Now look at the direction wanted and read the degrees on the compass dial. This is called shooting or taking an Azimuth or bearing. An Azimuth

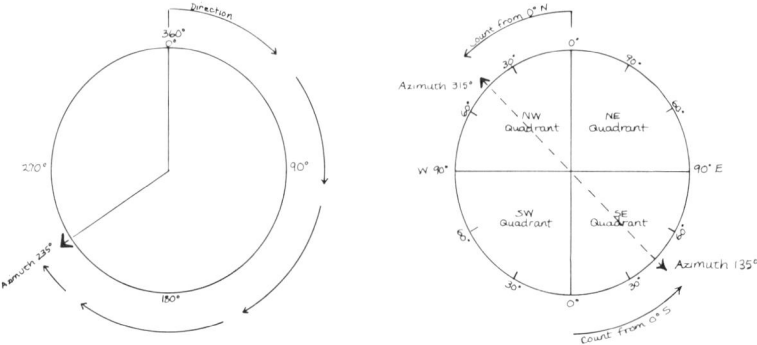

Fig. 2.6 The Azimuth Numbering System

is the line of direction measured in degrees in a clockwise manner from true north. This may sound technical, but it's really very simple. It is just the direction in degrees being traveled using a compass.

Using the compass can be divided into two sections: the first section here is concerned with finding the right direction on the ground from information given on your topographical map. To do this it is necessary to take a bearing first from the map using the four step technique.

THE FOUR-STEP TECHNIQUE

1. Place the compass on the map with the left edge along the desired line of travel. In other words, the route you will travel from your present location to your destination.

2. Turn the compass dial until the orienting lines on the transparent bottom are parallel with the grid lines of the map and north (N) points to north on the map (to the top of the map).

3. Set the magnetic variation by twisting the housing anti-clockwise to whatever the magnetic variation is.

4. Hold the compass in front of you and turn around until the red end of the compass needle points to north on the housing rim. This process is simple as saying 1, 2, 3, 4 and should become as natural to the backpacker as counting.

WHERE AM I?

The second part of compass work is concerned with finding out where you are on a map. This process is called triangulation. First, lay out the map and orient it using the compass to determine true north-south. Remember that the top of the map always points north. Select a vital landmark such as a high peak or a high tree. Take an azmath or a bearing on the peak. Next lay the compass on the map where the peak is shown. Draw a straight line with a pencil through the top of the peak and on the exact same bearing as the one found on the compass. Now repeat the whole operation using a different landmark. Where the two pencil lines intersect is the exact position on the map where the bearings were taken. That position will indicate where you are. Now that you can locate your position on the map by triangulation and can plot the direction that you need to go to reach your destination, all you need is practice. When in the field, follow the directions set on the compass, hold the compass in front of you with the direction of the travel arrow pointing straight ahead. Turn yourself while holding the compass at chest level until the north part of the compass needle covers the north arrow on the bottom of the housing. The direction of travel arrow now points to your destination. Pick a landmark in line with it, walk to that point and then repeat the process. Practice walking to an exact spot using only the compass. Set up a compass course and follow it for several miles. That's the best way to learn and the only way to remember these skills when they are needed. You might start by getting into a park or open field, establishing a starting point as a given landmark. Practice walking north for twenty paces and then turning east and walking another twenty paces. Turn south and walk a similar distance, then to the west for a final point of basis. If all the paces were the same length, you should end up at the exact spot where you started, having walked a perfect square course. If not, you did something wrong!

There's really nothing much to it except setting the correct direction on the compass and aligning the north marker with the needle and then following the direction of the travel arrow on the base plate. All field navigation consists of three quite elementary steps: orienting the map, determining a bearing, and following that bearing as you walk. There are of course some potential obstacles to your hike along nearly any given azmath. If you encounter a swamp or lake it's no problem to cite on a tree or some other prominent feature that lies across the obstacle on the proper course. Walk around the water to reach that landmark and again check your compass bearing. If you continue on the proper course from that landmark, you'll be heading along the correct azimuth. Remember if you alter your course exactly 90 degrees for a given number of paces, turn back to the original bearing until you pass the obstruction, then move the same number of paces to the opposite 90 degree side and continue to travel from that point, you will be on your exact bearing again.

ALTERNATE WAYS TO FIND DIRECTION

Every member of a backpacking party should be carrying a compass (see the list in Chapter 4 of the ten essentials). But in the event you are traveling alone and break your compass or lose it, there are several rustic methods which will allow you to find north.

The fact that the morning sun rises roughly east of you and sets roughly due west gives a general indication of the approximate directions of north, south, east, and west.

The seasons will cause fluxuation of the exact point of the solar path, but these directions are close enough for emergency navigation. At noon the sun will be almost due south of your position, so you'll be heading north with the noontime sun if it's to your back. Remember to allow for daylight savings time in making these calculations. If you have a watch, you can more accurately determine true north by the sun. Put a stick in the ground and mark the end of the shadow it casts at 10:00 a.m. Mark the shadow again at 2:00 p.m. Since each period is equidistant from local 12:00 or noon, measure the distance between the two shadow marks and divide it in half. The line from the base of the stick to this halfway point will point exactly north. Or if you wish, you can estimate directions during daylight hours by pointing the hour hand of your watch directly at the sun and noting the direction of 12:00 in the dial. With the hour hand pointed at the sun, south will be halfway between the hour hand and 12:00. (See Fig. 2.7) At night, you can find true north by simply locating the north star, Polaris. Polaris can be found by locating the familiar Big Dipper. (See Fig. 2.8) A line drawn through the outer two stars and extended about five times the distance between them will touch Polaris. The accompanying sketch shows this location. (See Fig. 2.9) However, hopefully you will take every precaution to not find yourself in the wilderness without a map or compass and particularly without the knowledge required to use them. There is no point in knowing which way is north if you don't know which way you must travel to reach your destination. A map gives the information you need and a compass will allow you to follow it. With these two tools, you can roam the unchartered backcountry and wilderness at will. Along with the proper techniques for overcoming the obstacles

S

PLUMBED

4

RADIUS – LENGTH
OF AM SHADOW

TIP OF AM
SHADOW

2

A AND B EQUAL

B

A

N

MARKER WHEN
PM SHADOW TOUCHES
RADIUS

S

N

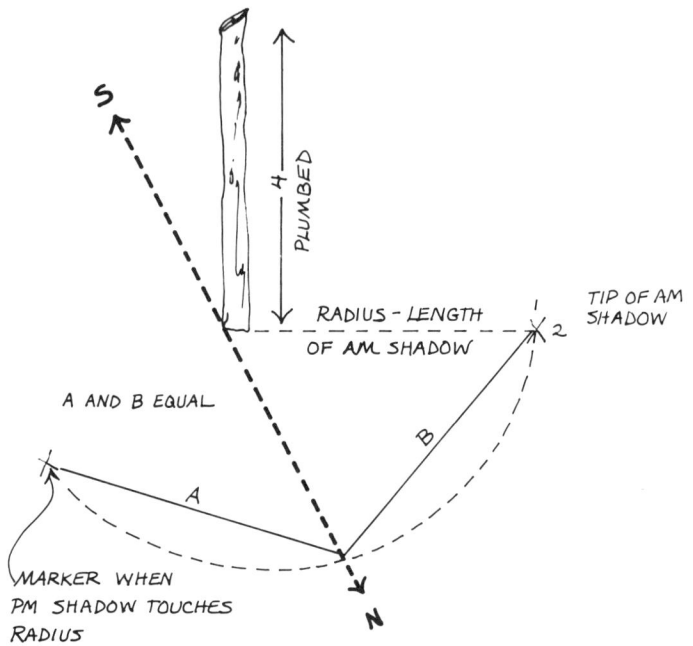

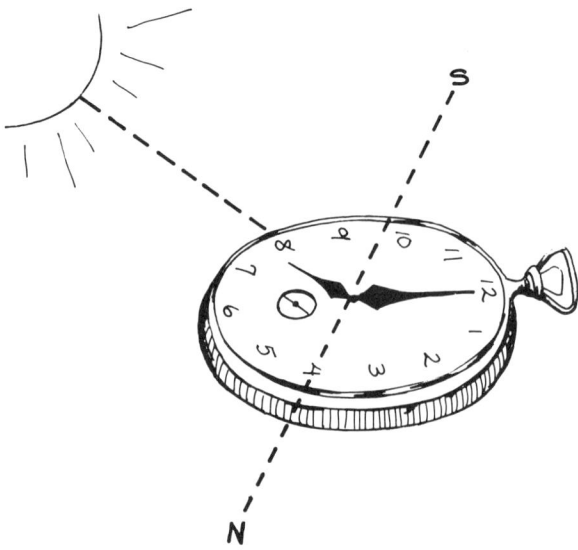

Fig. 2.7 Finding directions with watch and sun

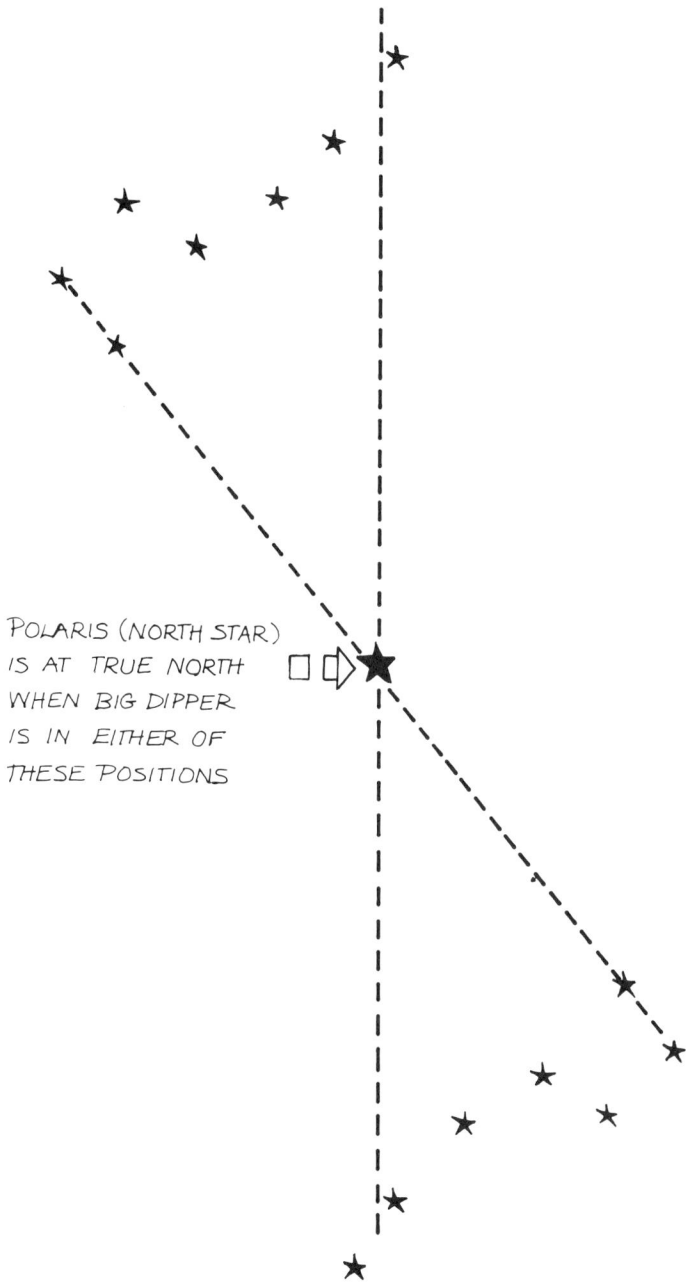

POLARIS (NORTH STAR)
IS AT TRUE NORTH
WHEN BIG DIPPER
IS IN EITHER OF
THESE POSITIONS

Fig. 2.8 Finding the North Star

along the way, these skills will unlock the very last door between you and the heart of the wilderness.

SOME CAUTIONS

Inasmuch as you've been walking all your life, you wouldn't think that a person would need much instruction in the art of hiking. But most of us have been walking on surfaces such as sidewalks, floors, stairways, trails, boardwalks, and carpeting. In cross country walking you'll need to watch out for steep angles, pine needles, slick roots, mossy rocks, wet trails, water crossings, and many

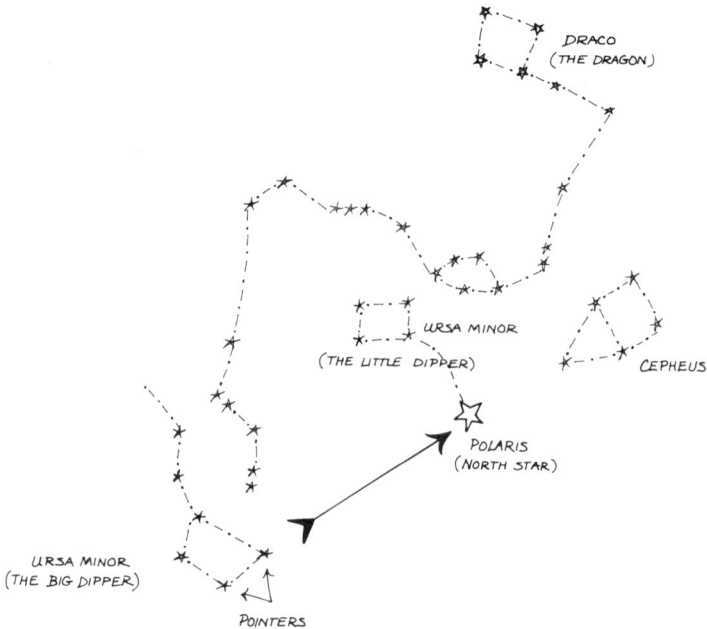

Fig. 2.9 Polaris and the Big Dipper

other different situations. The first and foremost rule in walking through the brush is pretty easy. That rule is watch where you put your feet. This is especially true as you are casually walking along, checking your compass, looking at scenery, watching an eagle flying overhead, and then suddenly find yourself several yards downhill trying to untangle from your pack. If you must look around, and not watch where you are walking, then do it from a stop. Cross country walking is largely a matter of common sense, but it does require more attention than when merely strolling along a smooth easy trail.

Prior to going on your trip, notify the proper authorities, family, and friends as to where the trail head will be, how long you'll be gone, and give an approximate time of your return. Although single backpacking can be a time for solitude and reflection, as usual, the buddy system is best. In case of emergencies, another individual along can be a great help. Try to meet the schedule that you proposed on your trip and upon returning, notify the authorities of your return and your friends as well. If you become lost or disoriented, it's better to sit tight and wait for a rescue team to come looking for you. In some instances, this is simply impossible. If you have no immediate prospect of rescue or you have failed to let anyone know where you are going, you'll have to find your way out of the woods. Immediate concerns should be providing yourself with sufficient water, keeping warm, avoiding fatigue, and keeping a positive mental attitude. Then think of ways to help a rescue or search party in any manner possible. Visible or audible signaling should be carried out at regular intervals. Many experienced backpackers carry a referee's whistle strictly as an emergency signaling device. In a pinch, you can make a good whistle from a supple willow. Smoke and fire are reasonably good visual signals in the wilderness. At night a flashlight can be used to signal passing aircraft or search planes. The international distress signal is a series of three signs of any kind. Three smudge fires, three whistles, or three flashes of a light. Try to move to a piece of high, clear ground where you will be spotted easier. There is especially one hard and fast rule that you should adhere to if you attempt to hike out and that is, **don't travel at night**. The importance of this advice is obvious.

The experienced backpacker is apt to be a good survivor on even the most difficult of circumstances. Hopefully, you will never find yourself in a survival situation. At any rate, if you do, you should seek shelter wherever it can be found, and protect yourself against illness and danger. When dire emergencies arise, do everything possible to keep yourself and your party alive and intact.

3 Equipment

WHAT'S NECESSARY

The techniques of camping along the trail have changed over the past few years. Twenty years ago it was perfectly acceptable to cut a few boughs for a mattress or to use saplings for tent poles or campfire sticks. Today, it just isn't feasible. With the millions of new campers and backpackers we now have, we would soon turn the wilderness into a wasteland. With the development of new and better equipment, it's not only easier to be completely self-sufficient, it's a lot more comfortable. More importantly, however, with the right equipment and techniques a backpacker can now pass through the loveliness of the forest without leaving a trace of his presence. Because of these advantages, it is most desirable and practical to carry everything you need into the wilderness and everything you use back out. Every member of the party should be adequately equipped with enough essential equipment to get along by themselves. Children generally are the only exception to the "every man for himself" rule. They usually aren't quite ready to shoulder a full load. Children should however, be provided with a small pack to carry their own trail snacks, socks and jacket, and other light items. Experience quickly teaches which things are needed and which things on a backpacking trip become excess baggage. The following list of outdoor equipment developed over the years by thousands of hikers comprise what might be classified as the ten essentials and is subscribed to by virtually every outdoor or hiking organization in the country. A lot of trial and error went into the selection of these vital items and you should carry them on every outing.

The list includes:

1. extra clothing
2. extra food
3. first aid kit
4. knife
5. flashlight
6. sunglasses
7. waterproof matches
8. fire starter
9. compass
10. map

Although equipment is generally chosen on the basis of personal taste, in assembling the group of ten essentials, consider the trip's length. On a simple one day hike, a very

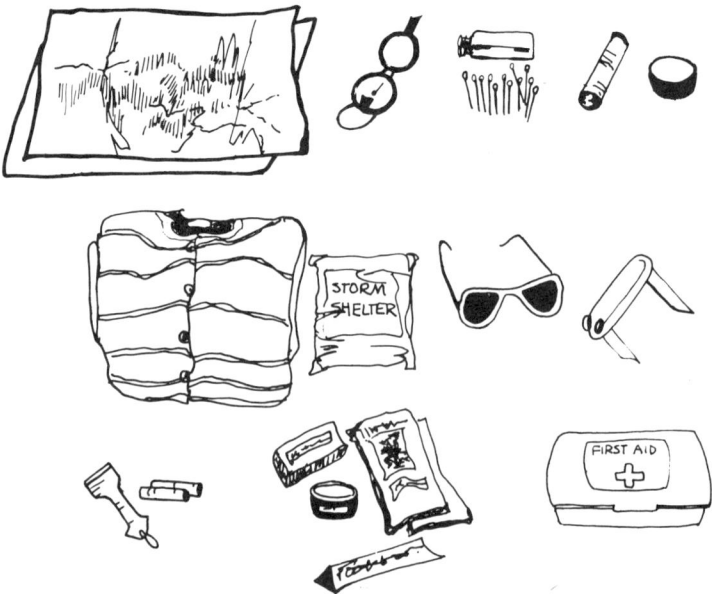

Fig. 3.0 The ten essentials

basic first aid kit will suffice. On a two-week trip, the kit would be expanded. These ten essentials will help protect you under almost any circumstance and they should be carried at all times.

It is difficult to try and list all of the equipment needed for various trips, however. Personal preference plays a big part in clothing the backpacker selects but if you hang around the trail head very long, you'll note that when the garb of experienced hikers is compared, there will be some very logical similarities that are apparent.

No matter what type of area you are planning on going into or how long you want to stay, the prepared backpacker is always concerned with five things.

1 — To be warm and comfortable (suitable clothing, shelter, and sleeping gear).

2 — To be fed (gear for cooking and eating, means of preparing meals, and food storage).

3 — To be clean (toilet articles).

4 — To have fun (recreational supplies, camera, fishing tackle, etc.)

5 — To carry all gear efficiently and to be able to handle emergencies that may arise.

The main difference between the veteran backpacker and the tenderfoot is not only experience, but attitude. When selecting equipment the experienced packer considers how many times per trip he will need or use the item, if it is worthy of its weight (low in bulk, practical, durable), and he will talk to other knowledgeable backpackers and read a wide selection of up-to-date books dealing with this field. He realizes there is no compromise for quality, and before including an item in his pack always asks, "Do I really need it?" Most of the more specialized equipment you will need can be found at any mountain shop or sporting goods store, as well as the less expensive Army-Navy surplus store. Many substitute items can be found in thriftshops or made at home from things already around the house. You can save up to one-half the cost of the more expensive items such as parka, pack, sleeping bag and tent, by assembling kits sold by Frostline, Cari Kit, and EMSKITS.

SHOPPING USING A PLAN

The chart on the following pages lists suggested equipment for the different length trips which may be taken, as well as specifying the basics for all backpacking outings and those items which should be carried by every individual, or which may be divided among the group. Each of these suggestions of course, should be adapted to individual or group needs, and much of the equipment listed is only optional. For short afternoon walks in summer sunshine or on broad trails, no equipment is really necessary, although full-day hikes do require some essentials. (See the column for one-day trips). The types of food you should bring, various methods of cooking and food preparation, and sample menus and recipes are included in the Cooking and Food section of this book. (Suggested Equipment List)

GETTING IT ALL TOGETHER

In order to be a successful backpacker, you must first be a skillful and knowledgeable hiker. Always walk with good posture, holding your head and chest high. Don't get too hot or cold when hiking in warm weather. If you are ever perspiring, you need to slow down since a slow and easy walking motion is the best course for warm weather excursions. The universal guideline, however, is to recognize your individual limitations and go at your own pace. Your heart, lungs, and muscles determine the time that you need to travel and in reality the distance to be traveled has very little bearing on your speed. Rest five to ten minutes every hour to rid your muscles of accumulated waste products. When traveling in a group, pace them according to the speed of the slowest hiker. Keep the group together, take an occasional head count and have someone guard the rear for stragglers. When figuring the distance you can cover on a trip, the general guideline for estimating your uphill speed is a half-mile per hour; for downhill, two to three miles per hour. Over flat terrain, two to three miles per hour; and through brush you will probably be slowed down to less than a half-mile per hour. For uphill travel, take shorter steps and short rest stops and when going downhill, slow

*Essentials to be carried by every person at all times. (May omit 1-2 for 1-day or overnight trip.)

ITEM	1-Day Trip	Over-Night Trip	2-Day Plus Trip	Dist. Among Group	COMMENTS/OPTIONAL	SUBSTITUTION(S)
SHELTER:						
Sweatshirt	X	X	X		Use in loose layer system as described in clothing section	Flannel shirt, sweater
Storm Shelter	X	X	X		Poncho type covering, emergency tarp, nylon or plastic, large enough for you plus pack to walk with	Parka, plastic garbage bag
Appropriate Clothing & Extra	X	X	X		See clothing section	
Sleeping bag w/stuff bag		X	X		Warm, not too heavy, include wool insert for winter. See section on sleeping gear.	
Foam Pad		X	X		Make sure has good loft (thickness). See section on sleeping gear	Air mattress — a lot heavier
Small Pillow		X	X		Optional	Fill stuff bag with extra jacket, clothes, etc.
Backpack Tent		X (opt)	X	X	Stormproof, lightweight, include poles, pegs, guy ropes, etc. See text section.	Plastic, cloth, or canvas lean-to
Rainfly		X (opt)	X (opt)	X	Depends on type of tent, essential in stormy weather.	4½' x 8' sheet plus nylon twine. 3 mil vinyl plastic or can use poncho.
Ground cover		X	X	X	Required for lean-tos, prevents tent floor abrasion. Polyethylene sheet (7' x 8') for two.	Poncho, storm shelter
COOKING:						
Personal Utensils		X	X		Stainless steel or plastic, not aluminum maybe a set like boyscouts — supplement with coathanger cooking stick.	Plastic ware, regular silverware, or just get along with a spoon.
Plate, cup, bowl		X	X		Plastic is good, not aluminum cup, Scout cook or "mess" kit, cup with measuring marks is handy.	Can use group cook kit, use only cup, or make out of foil

EQUIPMENT LIST (cont.)

ITEM	1-Day Trip	Over-Night Trip	2-Day Plus Trip	Dist. Among Group	COMMENTS/OPTIONAL	SUBSTITUTION(S)
Large Cook Kit		X (opt)	X (opt)	X	Sigg Tourist Cooker, Nesting Billies, Teflon or Steel fry pan, nylon spatula, lids, replace indiv. sets	Make out of tin cans (#10). Lids out of foil, boil watering metal cup. Indiv. sets may replace
Stirring Spoon		X (opt)	X (opt)	X (opt)	Wooden, long-handled, depends on menu.	Shaped stick, handle of other utensil.
Can Opener		X (opt)	X (opt)	X (opt)	Maybe optional depending on menu	Maybe part of knife, Boy Scout or GI type.
Foil, Paper towels		X (opt)	X	X	Both are essential, many uses, saves on dishes	
Matches		X (opt)	X	X	In waterproof packet, large amount for cooking. Waterproof if desired with paraffin wax.	
Hot Mitten		X (opt)	X	X	Asbestos is best, especially useful over open fire. Supplement with pot gripper.	Hot Pad Pliers
1-burner stove		X (opt)	X	X	Weighs 1-2 lbs. Either gasoline, kerosene, butane, propane, or alcohol. Depends on menu. See section on backpack stoves.	To warm food — canned heat "Sterno" or heatabs type stove.
Grill or Grate		X (opt)	X	X	Could be cake rack, not more than 1/2 lb. 5" width, to fit in pack (in plastic bag) — may be optional if no open fire, must be metal.	Two rocks close together with smooth surfaces to set pans upon.
Pot scrubbers			X	X	Scouring pad or nylon netting to loosen food, particles and charcoal, makes things a lot easier.	Tri-Soapy Towel, unopened pine cone, sand and gravel
Dish Soap			X	X	Means of cutting grease, liquid type is the best.	Tri-Soapy Towel
Salt and Pepper Shaker			X	X	Two compartment plastic container with snap-on lids. May substitute other condiments.	Securely locked plastic bags.

Item					Comments	Materials / Substitutes
Sugar Dispenser Vegelene	X	X			Depends on menu, tight covered containers can put in polyethylene units.	Oil will replace vegelene. Brown sugar instead of white or honey.
Wire Coathanger	X	X	X (opt)		Pull into a square and cover with foil to make frying pan or plate, or make long handles for pans, etc.	Piece of wire
Food Containers	X	X	X (opt)	X (opt)	Polyethylene bags, boxes, squeeze tubs, bottles, jars, egg boxes, etc. at mountaineer shops	Baggies, Ziplocks, Tupperware, etc.
Sufficient* food plus extra	X	X	X (substantial lunch)		Always should be some left over in case of emergency. See section on cooking. Most people tend to pack too much.	
TOILET ARTICLES:						
Washcloth	X	X			Optional — keep in plastic wrap — nice to have.	Wash N Dries, Paper towels, etc.
Towel, soap	X	X (opt)	X (opt)		Small cloth towel (not bath towel), keep in separate plastic bags.	Re-usable paper towel, handi-wipes, etc., 1 all-purpose towel, dish towel, tri-soapy towels, half bar of soap or liquid.
Toothbrush, paste	X	X (opt)	X (opt)		Put brush in plastic bag or case, toothpaste in foil.	Baking soda
Comb, brush	X	X	X (opt)		Pocket comb is the handiest option. Both are optional	
Shaving Gear	X				Optional	
Toilet paper	X	X	X (opt)		Called "mountain money". Keep wrapped in plastic. Plan to have enough.	Kleenex
Kleenex	X	X			Wrap in plastic wrap or bag. Optional.	Handkerchief, paper towels, toilet paper.
Small Mirror	X	X			Polished steel with cover. Optional	

ITEM	1-Day Trip	Over-Night Trip	2-Day Plus Trip	Dist. Among Group	COMMENTS/OPTIONAL	SUBSTITUTION(S)
Nailfile			X	X	Optional	Emery board, pocket nailcutters.
Sanitary Supplies			X		Minimum of two per female. Altitude affects everyone's cycle.	
Lipsalve	X (opt)	X (opt)	X		For dry skin, prevention of peeling, blisters, etc. Chapstick, vasoline, Noxema.	Sunburn preventative (Sea & Ski)
2 clothes pins			X	X	Optional — can make clothes line with rope.	
Sunglasses*	X (opt)	X (opt)	X		Dark, for sun, snow, desert, alpine regions, etc. Prefer enclosed slides with innerchanging base.	Prescription or clip-ons for those with glasses.
Insect Repellent	X (opt)	X	X	X	Decreases amount of bites, lotions or foam, increases year-round comfort. OFF, Cutter Cream, etc.	
Sunburn Preventative	X (opt)	X (opt)	X (opt)	X	For wind, sun, high elevations, snow. Prevent early. Don't wait for red or hot skin to use it.	Anything for dry skin depending on skin sensitivity.
Wash 'N Dries	X (opt)	X (opt)	X	X	Very handy, especially for families with children. Keep fresh, old ones loose moisture.	Any towelettes individually wrapped with detergent & antiseptic & solvent.
RECREATION:						
License & Fishing Tackle	X	X	X		Current license, keep hooks, etc., wrapped separately. Optional — see section on fishing — know regulations	
Snowshoes	X	X	X		Binding needs to fit shoes, being in good repair. Optional. And the right size. See section on Winter Activities.	
Ski pole(s)	X	X	X		To help with snow backpacking. Optional — See section on Winter Activities.	Snow pined poles

Item			Description	Notes
Binoculars	X	X	Good with magnification of 6 or 8, weighs ½ lb. Optional	Opera glasses may serve the purpose. Optional
Wind meter/pocket thermometer	X	X	Optional — to keep track of the weather or just for a hobby.	
Watercolor Pad & Paints	X	X	Optional	Sketch pad and pencil
Tree, shrub, moss, flower manual	X	X	Optional — may be part of combined nature book.	Scout manual
Insect, Bird, or Animal Guide	X	X	Optional — may be part of combined nature book.	Scout manual
Rock & Minerals or Astronomy Book	X	X	Optional — may be part of combined nature book.	Scout manual
Magnifying Glass/Butterfly Net	X	X	Optional — observation purposes	
Camera, kite, games, etc.	X	X	Bring extra film, cubes, batteries; desirable to be able to take pictures. Optional — pocket chess set, paperback, etc.	Make up own games, write a poem or story, whatever you like.
GENERAL: Map(s)*	X	X	Required for all trips taken in the wilderness. Carry in polyethylene bag for protection. Know how to read them (See Orienteering).	
Fire Starter	X (opt)	X	Commercially manufactured items that are impregnated with chemicals that assist in starting wood or charcoal fires (fire ribbon, tablets, etc.)	Steel wool with batteries. Plumbers candle, flint stick, metal watch, flint and steel, etc. Also piece of candle will light.
Extra Plastic Bags	X (opt)	X	Have many uses — to carry trash out in, put wet clothes in, mix food in, etc. (Ziplocks, Baggies)	
Small Shovel	X	X	"Garden type" — steel or aluminum blade. Optional. To put out fires, bury ashes, etc.	Kitchen scoop may work for loose dirt.

EQUIPMENT LIST (cont.)

ITEM	1-Day Trip	Over-Night Trip	2-Day Plus Trip	Dist. Among Group	COMMENTS/OPTIONAL	SUBSTITUTION(S)
Rope			X		Approximately 50 feet — not clothesline type. Nylon cordage is light, strong and weatherproof, but stretches, is slippery and most expensive. Can use to lash boots or backpacks in emergency.	Hemp rope is good for all around use. String may be of temporary use.
Flashlight*	X	X	X		Check batteries before leaving, bring extra cells and bulb. 2 cells for C or D type flashlight.	2-AA mallory flashlights (pocket size) + 4 extra alkaline cells. Can warm "dead" cells for more life.
Pocket Knife*	X	X	X		Always carry on body, make sure sharpened before leaving — Boy Scout or Swiss Army type. Use for eating, first aid, emergency fire, etc.	
Water Canteen	X	X	X		Carry on body or belt, should bring 2-one quart containers for longer trips (metal type, plastic, etc.)	Can supplement with a collapsible plastic water bottle = 2-7 oz.
Compass*	X	X	X		Clear base with grid lines and moveable base. Carry on body, know how to use, (See Orienteering). Polaris or Boy Scout models are good.	Sun compass, stars, etc., only in emergency. (See Survival Section)
Matches in Metal Container*	X	X	X		Carry on person, water and windproof "safety matches". Screw on waterproof-type container (Boy Scout model)	Aluminum film container. Dip matches in paraffin wax to waterproof.
Pencil & Paper	X (opt)	X (opt)	X	X	Necessary for triplay, diary, letters, messages, etc. Small notebook is handy.	
Watch	X (opt)	X	X	X	Don't bring a good one, need a few per group. Keep one in car for trip home.	Sun dial in emergency.

Item				Notes	Alternatives / Substitutes
Stainless Steel Cup	X (opt)	X		For getting water easily while hiking, Comerwal, wipe handle, can use for small pan (Sierra cup)	Collapsible pocket cup or paper cup.
Hatchet		X	X	Optional — usually unnecessary, use piece of garden hose to protect blade, know how to use. (See Camp Tools)	Hand axe or ice axe.
Small Saw			X	Optional — usually unnecessary, folding type is handy, handle safely (See Camp Tools)	
Sharpening Tool			X	Optional — should own one but don't need to bring. Mill file of 8'' to sharpen ax, or whetstone for knife.	Hone-used to sharpen cutting tools
Tarp for Woodpile		X	X	Optional	Groundcloth, poncho, etc.
Water-proofing Material			X	Optional — Mainly of use during winter (Snow Seal). Especially necessary for leather boots.	Wrap stocking feet in plastic bags.
Back-packing Handbook	X	X	X	Optional — preferably lightweight and informative.	Trail guidebook, Scout manual, etc.
Pack Frame and Bag	X (opt)	X	X	Fits and is in good repair, bag needs to attach well to frame (See Backpacks)	For 1-day trip can use bikepack, day pack, or mucksack.
Day Pack		X	X	Optional — handy for afternoon hikes. Nylon material with outside pockets is the best.	Bikepack or rucksack. Can bring child carrier.
Repair Kit		X	X	Optional — In a plastic bag — 2-inch rip-stop cloth type, webbing, nuts, bolts, heavy thread and needle, rings, clevis pins, awl, wipes, etc., for pack, tent, boots, etc.	
Extra Lashing Cord		X	X	Optional — mainly to repair snowshoes	Part of nylon cordage (50 feet)
Small Scripture Book	X	X	X	Keep in bags for protection. Optional.	Thoughtbook, poems, or uplifting paperback.

EQUIPMENT LIST (cont.)

ITEM	1-Day Trip	Over-Night Trip	2-Day Plus Trip	Dist. Among Group	COMMENTS/OPTIONAL	SUBSTITUTION(S)
Personal First Aid Kit*	X	X	X		(See suggested contents for First Aid Kit)	
Wire and Wirecutters			X	X	Optional. Odd and End uses	Pliers are handy. See wire coathanger.
Rubber Bands			X	X	Many uses — close plastic bags, keep similar items together, emergency repairs, etc. OPTIONAL	String, paperclips, etc.

your pace and check your footing. During short stops it is best to remain standing to minimize fatigue. Always stay on the designated trail and frequently verify your position on the map. Avoid loose rocks, dirt slides, snakes and poisonous plants along the trail. Remember that high elevations may cause altitude sickness because there is less oxygen in the air. It's wise to walk slowly and steadily and from time to time munch some of the candy or other quick energy foods. A hiker can expend 4,000 to 6,000 calories per day, depending upon the weather and the terrain he's covering, and this energy needs to be replaced. An efficient precautionary measure is to drink three to four quarts of water or juice each day to prevent dehydration. In moderate temperatures, try to drink warm liquids so that you don't use essential inner heat to warm them for your body's needs. Always watch the sky and be weather conscious. Respect the terrain, stay on the trail, and don't hike in dangerous conditions. Rain, blizzard, whiteouts, dense fog, darkness, desert sun, and lightning are all hazardous to your health. For lightning, stay in low unexposed areas away from single trees, water and rock outcrops. In dense woods, lie down where you are if no shelter is available. Appoint a foul weather leader to call a halt to the hike before the least protected member of the group becomes exhausted or goes into violent shivers. Don't underestimate "cool" air temperatures and never allow chilling. Be aware of wind chill which is the cooling power of wind driven upon the human body. In the winter, freezing, frostbite, chilblains, snow blindness, over fatigue and dampness are your enemies. Wind is extremely dangerous during the winter months because it refrigerates wet clothes by evaporating moisture from the surface. Water chill is very dangerous. You should always ask how cold will the water be against my body.

Proper hiking manners include leaving any gates open or closed as you find them, protecting the animals, and not throwing rocks endangering humans or animal life. Any discussion of hiking must include a mention of proper foot care. If your feet get wet, stop and change your socks immediately. Keep your feet clean, your socks washed and your shoes dry. Toenails should be kept short and cut straight across the top. As soon as you feel any discomfort such as rubbing, binding, or pinching, stop and find out the cause and remedy it before going on. At the end of a day's hike, wash your feet in cold salt water, massage them, and twist the arches for optimum foot refreshment.

4 Personal Gear & Pack

CLOTHING

There are some specific guidelines for the selection of clothing regardless of temperature or terrain. Always choose clothing which is easy to adjust and has the proper insulation and ventilation for the current weather conditions. The backpacker should never hesitate to put on or to take off the proper clothing when needed. In general, garments should not be tight fitting, and when purchasing or selecting jackets, raingear, sweatshirts, etc., you should consider the efficiency of the item in terms of the weight units that you will be carrying because of it.

Jackets, especially those for cold or windy weather, should have excellent loft, be permeable to body moisture, lightweight, easily compressed for stowage and carrying, and allow plenty of freedom of movement. For adjustability they should have as many of the following features as possible:

1 — Hoods closing with a drawstring or velcro tape, and that snap on below the collar if removable

2 — Double insulated neck areas, snug collars and cuffs with snaps, elastic, or velcro

3 — A front zipper which can open from the top and/or bottom

4 — A drawstring at the bottom, and above the hips if a longwaisted style.

During the summer, proper clothing helps you retain your body moisture by not letting it evaporate so fast that you get only part of its cooling effect. (A naked body dehydrates much faster than a clothed one.) Light clothing also reflects or turns away the heat of the sun, and is especially good for keeping out the hot desert air. While in the heat you need to ration your perspiration through adjusting your clothing and body movement, and not your water. In the winter you can control your body heat loss with your clothes by collecting the moisture from the skin layer (or innermost layer of clothing), and passing it to consecutive outer layers, which will then soak it up through a wool shirt or jacket. When out in cold weather, keep your head covered and your feet dry to avoid chilling the entire body. Be sure to use your head — cover it when cold and uncover it to avoid sweating. Keep the torso warm in order to heat the toes and fingers. Always carry instant body shelter from wind and wetness, and whenever windy, put it on. In an emergency you can pad your clothing with an insulation of moss, paper, etc. In order to prevent hypothermia, the number one killer of out door recreationalists, every backpacker needs to:

Keep clothing Clean
Avoid Overheating
Wear Clothing in Loose layers
Keep clothing Dry

The advantages and disadvantages of each of the various materials available in outdoor wear should be considered when selecting clothing items. Cotton is very comfortable, lightweight, and warm when dry, but mats, absorbs moisture, and is worse than useless when it is wet. Most cotton combinations breathe easily, and are light, strong, and durable, but are less warm than 100% cotton garments. Wool, or reprocessed wool absorbs little moisture, doesn't mat, and retains its warmth even when wet by drying from the inside out. A wool and nylon mixture is much more durable than pure wool. Down-filled clothing gives a lot of loft, is easy to compress for storage, light weight, and very warm, but when wet, loses virtually all insulation value and takes days to dry. Polyester or dacron retains most of its insulation ability even when drenched

58

and is quickly dried by body heat alone.

Always use the **loose layer system** of clothing for both summer and winter backpacking trips. This consists of easy on and off type garments with various layers of clothing being utilized to trap dead air insulation inbetween. The first layer closest to the skin should be a cotton T-shirt, or undershirt, with a light cotton shirt over it. The next layer should be a button or zippered up long-sleeved shirt, windbreaker, vest, sweater, or down jacket, depending on the weather, to regulate heat. The third layer during the winter would consist of a large, long-waisted wool shirt of a heavy-tight weave, (wool should always be worn over down to absorb moisture). The last or outermost layer should consist of some sort of rain gear and windstopper, including a water-proofed type of hood or head protection. Use the clothing list on the following page to help compile your backpacking wardrobe. (Suggested List of Clothing)

BOOTS

Backpackers consider their boots to be the most important single item of equipment they own. While the casual stroller can wear tennis shoes or waffle stompers, the serious backpacker can allow no compromise in either quality or fit of his boots. There's good reason for this. Everything he does, every move he makes, depends on his feet. Therefore, in choosing quality, style, and design of one's boots, the choice should be based on the following three critical areas:

1. The boots should always be made of leather.
2. They should always have thick, lug soles.
3. They should always offer solid ankle support. Whether they are low cut with a cuff or collar or are high toppers, the best of both styles should be formed of a single piece of leather requiring only one seam up the heel. This cut reduces the chance of the boot leaking in wet weather since there are no sewn in seams across the instep or toes. The lugs of the soles of the shoes should be slightly tapered so that they have release grooves that allow mud and snow to be rejected with each step. The soles may be attached to the boot by a variety of methods. It could be sewn on or it may be cemented. Cemented soles offer a

SUGGESTED CLOTHING LIST

ITEM	COLD WEATHER	OPTIONAL/COMMENTS	SUBSTITUTIONS(S)
Hiking or trail boots	Rubberized or water-proofed leather. Use felt sole inserts.	Should have strong sole, be proper fitting, broken-in; hugs arch and heel, prevents friction and allows toes to spread. Polish leather to keep it pliable. Break in before leaving.	Sturdy and comfortable shoes (not tennis shoes). For cold — wrap stocking feet in baggies or plastic wrap.
Hat or cap	Use wool cap in winter. Hat to protect against sun may be optional.	For warm weather have it brimmed or with a bill for sun and wind protection. Use cap to keep head warm when cool.	For temporary use — waterproof plastic bag that is slit on the side and fits over the head.
Socks	Bring more pairs of wool ones. Tube socks are nice.	Bring one heavy pair/day of wool ones; wear a pair of white nylon socks against the skin. Dont't wear so many that cut off circulation. Bring extra pairs.	
Long pants with belt	Work pants or pair of ski powder ones. Should be proper fit and length.	No cuffs, sturdy jeans will work for summer. Bring a spare pair in case yours get wet (can be light rubberized or plastic pair). Wear a Scout, canvas belt (not a good one).	Not double knits or shorts for wear on the trail.
Underclothing	Thermal is great for cold. Fishnet works.	Bring extra sets in case you get wet.	Extra t-shirts or shorts.
Swimwear	Not needed.	Optional — trunks or swimsuit. Check out water for hazards **first**.	Shorts and t-shirt.
Light footwear	Down booties — heavy outdoor pair and/or soft sleeping pair for warmth.	Optional — nice to rest feet after a hike. Lounge slippers or moccasins.	Tennis shoes — only to rest in.
Shirts	Wear t-shirts plus wool shirts (bring extra).	White or light colored long-sleeved, buttoned or zippered front, plus a t-shirt. Full collar and neck button.	

60

ITEM	COLD WEATHER	OPTIONAL/COMMENTS	SUBSTITUTION(S)
Neckerchief	Warm scarf (wool).	Optional — good for neck protection. Make handkerchief hat, tie around hair, makes emergency triangle bandage.	Bandana or large hankerchief.
Parka or rain coat	Light with hood. Covers head, neck, body, and legs.	Full-cut, full-length and waterproof. Protects against wind-driven rain. Test at home. Not plastic or cotton; nylon, polyurethane coated nylon is best.	A poncho will work if necessary — poor in the wind.
Jacket	Heavy jacket (wool) or down.	Medium weight usually depending on the weather — down, polyester, or nylon.	Sweater if necessary — too heavy to pack in far.
Face mask	Wool bandana	Optional — loose fitting ear and neck cover.	Neckband and/or earband.
Gloves or mittens	Wool or ski mittens. Use rubber pair of gloves for snow work.	Bring 2 pairs to be safe — use to work in and for warmth. Also prevents blisters.	For winter — regular gloves with wool inserts. Can make emergency ones with plastic bags and black masking tape.
Canvas gaiters	Short or long style mainly for winter use. Keeps water from getting in shoes or under clothes.	Make by wrapping paper around each leg; then a layer of cloth, then sew in grommets to tie on.	

61

bit more flexibility in walking but generally cannot be replaced when worn out. Sewed on soles can be replaced by any competent shoemaker. (See Fig. 4.0)

Even if you were to select the finest boots, they will be utterly useless to you on the trail if they don't fit properly. We recommend that you go to a store where you can try the boots on before you buy them. Once good fitting boots have been chosen and broken in, be sure to give them the periodic maintenance they need to remain supple, water resistant and comfortable. Follow the manufacturer's recommendations for applying wax, silicon, grease or oil. Although hiking boots are the mainstay of the pedestrian wardrobe, they should be accompanied by a second pair of shoes. These can be high top gym shoes, or even deck shoes. They're nice to have for wearing around the camp while the boots are drying and in a pinch they can be worn down the trail as a substitute for a damaged pair of boots. Generally, a good rule of thumb, is to purchase the very best pair of boots you can afford. Along with the boots, seriously consider adding a pair of nylon gaiters. These are zip-on waterproof leggings that are anchored with a strap under the foot and extend to the upper calf. In rough weather they keep

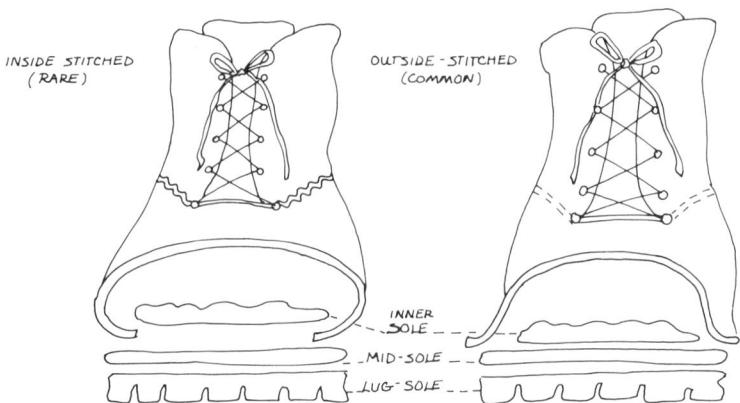

INSIDE STITCHED (RARE)

OUTSIDE-STITCHED (COMMON)

INNER SOLE

MID-SOLE

LUG-SOLE

Fig. 4.0 The hiking boot

socks and legs dry and protect against rain, mud and snow, poison ivy and poison oak. They are relatively inexpensive, very comfortable to wear, and the added protection is worth the cost.

SELECTION AND CARE OF SLEEPING GEAR

Your sleeping equipment mainly consists of a sleeping bag plus everything you might use for insulation from the ground. There should always be as much thickness under you as there is over you. The sleeping bag itself is the most important and usually the most expensive piece of camping gear. It is mainly built for warmth and prevention of body heat loss, and always needs to be in good condition, with the zipper working. You need to handle the zipper carefully and slowly so that it doesn't jam or tear the bag. When the zipper is difficult to operate, apply soap or a coating of light lubricating oil to the full length of the zipper or you may work it loose with a needle when only stuck.

Whatever type of sleeping bag you have, you'll eventually need to get a bag cover for both the bag and sleeping pad, which needs to be waterproof except for a strip on top to allow moisture to escape. Especially be careful when purchasing a new sleeping bag — you get what you pay for and bargain bags will not adequately meet your needs. There are seven specific qualities of the sleeping bag which need to be considered when selecting the appropriate bag for your use.

1. **Fill** — The possibilities of filler materials which are appropriate for backpacking range from the fairly new polyester or fiberfill or the fiberfill and down combination ("fiberdown"), up to the very best quality duck or goose down feathers, with the "eiderdown" (minimum of 80% down) and the Prime White Northern Goose Down being the most expensive kinds of fill available. Quality down provides 25% more insulation than polyester, and consequently a dacron bag must be one or two pounds heavier than a down bag to provide equal warmth. Whatever fill is used, however, needs to be evenly distributed throughout the bag and sewn in such a way as

to keep it compartmented that way. Don't get a sewn-through type of stitching which allows for many "cold spots." The slant tube or laminated style is the best for preserving the natural warmth of the fill.

2. **Loft** — This is the thickness of the insulation, which determines up to 60% the degree of warmth of the bag. It is measured as the space between the inner and outer covers of the bag, and is partially determined by the amount of filler utilized. The fluffier the loft, the higher the insulation value, because the best insulation is the air imprisoned in the bag covering, where the fill deadens the air flow. A 1½ to 2 inch loft of goose down will stay warm at around 40° F and is sufficient for mild climates or warm sleepers. Allow ¼ inch for every 10° below that, up to around 3 inches for very cold weather. In most conditions a bag that will still be warm down to around 25° F is ideal. A 2½ lb. down bag with a 3 inch loft is equivalent in warmth to a 3 lb. polyester bag with a 2¾ inch loft. Although down has more insulation value, the fiberfill bag drys very quickly and keeps its loft even when wet. Usually the deciding factor between a dacron or down sleeping bag will be the degree of wetness (the humidity and raininess) you expect to encounter. Polyester is generally the best choice for children.

3. **Construction** — This term refers mainly to the cover material of the bag. It needs to be water repellant but not waterproof, so that it can breathe and lose the body moisture which is collected from inside the bag. The outer fabric needs to be loose to allow the down or other type of fill to expand. It also needs to be lightweight, soft, and stain and abrasion resistant. Nylon (either taffeta or rip-stop) is easy breathing, wind resistant, and is the lightest and strongest of the various types of fabrics which are used. It also allows sleeper movement and turning without having the bag cling.

4. **Weight** — This factor becomes more important as the time out on the trail increases. People will therefore buy the more expensive down filled bag because it has less bulk and weight per degree of provided warmth than any other type of fill. During the summer a bag should never

weigh more than 4½ to 5½ lbs. (4 lbs. for down and 5 lbs. for polyester).

5. **Closure** — The zipper and/or snaps which are used to open and close the sleeping bag are considered in this category. The less the amount of zipper, the less the "cold spot" area and the lighter the overall weight. A zipper allows you to ventilate the bag according to the weather, and is therefore more versatile for various temperature ranges. Variations in zippers include half-length or full-length, one or two way, and top or side of the bag location. Nylon zippers do not conduct heat, freeze, or rip the shell fabric, and are light, self-lubricating, self-repairing, and take corners and angles well. Over-size or heavy duty zippers are the most dependable, and a two-way or two-slide zipper is convenient. A down filled tube (draft tube) needs to cover the zipper to prevent heat loss. If two bags are going to be zipped together, the zipper should go around the outside, and not up and down the center. Use a toggle or card-block for easy opening of the drawstring.

6. **Compressability** — Also known as recovery power, this refers to the ability of a bag to spring out to full expansion after being crushed. A bag needs to be easily compressable to increase packing ease as well as to be able to retain shape and insulation value after stuffing. Down is the easiest type bag to compress.

7. **Shape** — Sleeping bags are made in various shapes to meet individual preferences. The warmest design is the mummy bag, which is contoured to the body and may be closed by a drawstring to leave only the nose and mouth exposed to cold air. This bag would best suit those who don't need room to move around in, and don't mind having the bag move with you. The "Barrell" bag is square-cut at the top and is 10° colder, as well as much heavier than the mummy style, (although it does allow more freedom of body movement). The roomiest and heaviest style-cut bag is the rectangular shaped with no top closure, which is 20° colder than the mummy type. A tapered rectangular bag will save some weight while allowing for more room for movement, thus combining two of the major ad-

vantages of the other designs of sleeping bags. A good rule of thumb is the smaller the inside area of a bag, the warmer it will sleep. (See Fig. 4.1)

When making the final decision to purchase a quality sleeping bag, one also needs to consider body length compared to bag length (allowing extra room for neck-stretching and flexing toes), cost (it is usually wise to get the highest quality you can afford), and warmth (how much is really needed as opposed to how warm is the bag).

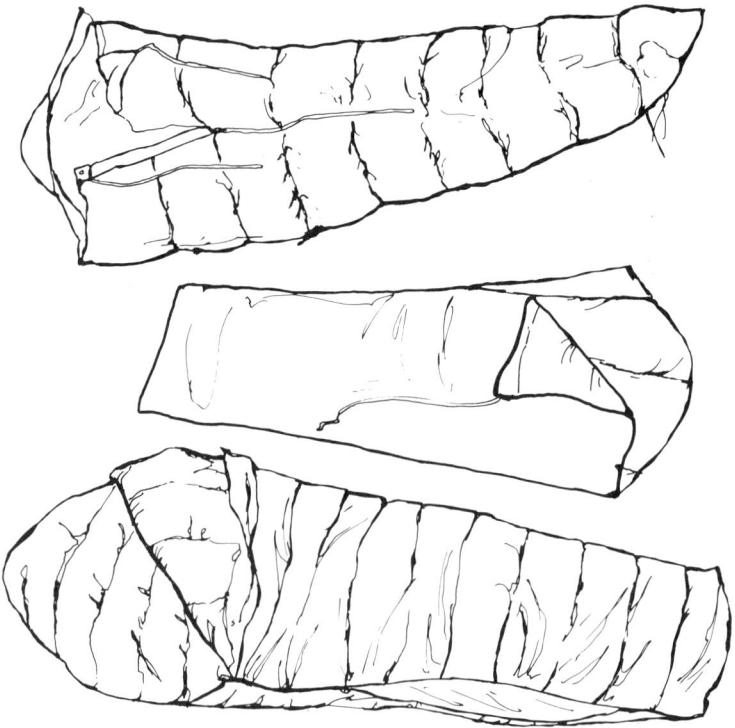

Above: with half-length top zipper. Middle: child's bag with half-length side zipper. Below: with full-length, two-way side zipper.

Fig. 4.1 Representative mummy bags

PROPER CARE OF SLEEPING BAGS

A good quality bag will last a long time with a minimum of care. Keep your bag aired frequently while in use, and in the sun's rays, to sterilize and refluff the filling. Old bed sheets or linens made of nylon, cotton flannel, or cotton-polyester may be used to keep the inside cleaner and prolong the life of the bag. Always keep away from sparks and campfires and clean the bag before it becomes too dirty. If the bag is of proper quality, it can be washed to keep it soft and fluffy. A polyester bag can be machine washed using a gentle or permanent press cycle, or even be hand-washed if preferred. Heavily soiled areas will need to be pre-scrubbed with a minimum amount of non-detergent soap. Rinse thoroughly, and dry in a dryer set on low, (since excessive heat will damage the fabric). For best results, only hand-wash a down bag according to instructions from the manufacturer. It is safest never to dry-clean your sleeping bag since the solvents which are used are toxic, and may be fatal if the fumes which often cling to the material are inhaled. Most bags that are now made for the backpacker don't need to be "rolled", but rather are "stuffed" into a "stuff bag." (See Fig. 4.2)

First the sleeping pad is stuffed in so that it circles the inside perimeter of the "stuff bag." Then stuff one corner of the sleeping bag down into the bottom, and slowly stuff in the rest of the bag and pull the drawstring of the "stuff bag" to close. For other types of bags, fold the bag lengthwise in half, and then roll from the bottom up, making as tight a bundle as possible, or you may even roll it into a "horse collar" shape to tie around your pack. The sleeping bag should always be unrolled and out of the stuff bag when at home and not in use, so that it can air out and the fill is allowed to expand. When renting a bag, turn it wrong side out, have it air out in the sun, and insist on a clean bag sheet from the out-fitter.

Sleeping Pads

Always keep some kind of ground sheet and/or pad underneath the bag, for both the care of the bag as well as to increase the comfort and warmth of the sleeper. The foam pad is the most popular and effective of the various types of ground insulation which are used by the back-

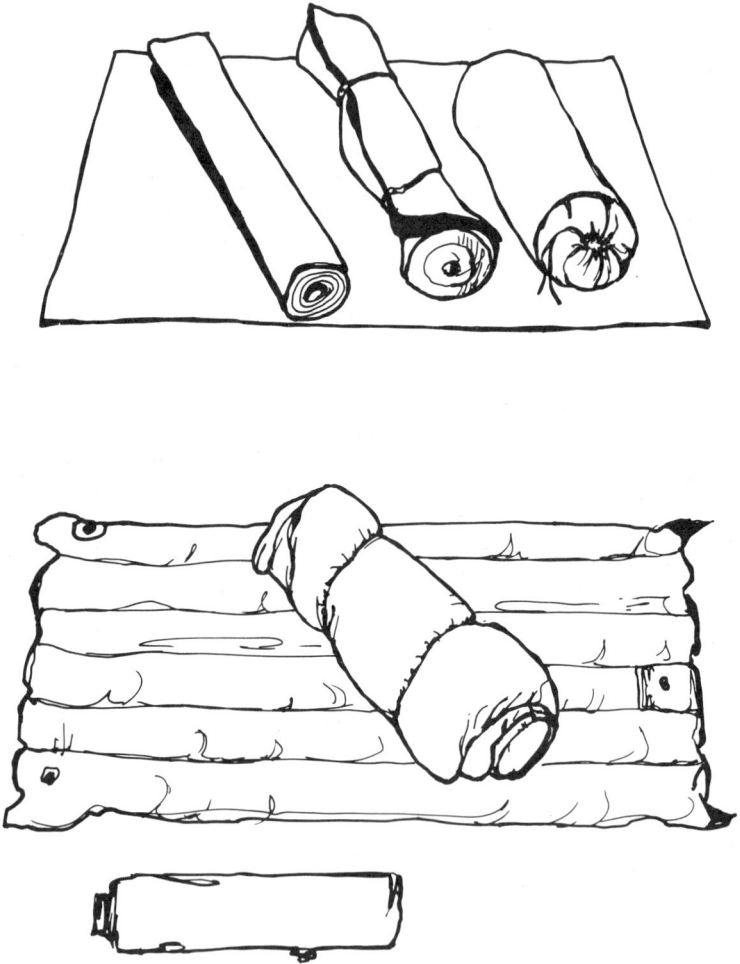

Above: sleeping bag in stuff bag. 1½-inch urethane sleeping pad, and ¼-inch ensolite pad — displayed on an ensolite pad spread out for use. Below: nylon air mattress, shoulders-to-hips length, inflated and deflated.

Fig. 4.2 Sleeping bags

packer. The "ensolite" pad which is closed-cell and dense, watertight, and rolls into a very small unit, usually comes in 3/8" or 1/2" thickness, extends for about 3/4 of your body length (28" x 56"), weighs around 1 3/4 pounds, and is a very light weight means of keeping out ground moisture. Also, either the white polyethylene pad of 1/4" thickness, 24" x 72" area, and 3/4 pound weight, or the blue-foam polyethylene of 3/8" thickness, 24" x 48" area, and 6 ounces weight also serves very well for the average kind of trip. For extra cushioning, softness and resiliency, a urethane foam pad of 1 1/2" to 2" thickness, extending from the width of the shoulders to the lower torso (24" x 48") and weighing 1 1/4 pounds is very popular. Also called "polyether", this type pad is open-celled, which means it will sponge up water from the ground, is very bulky, and is not as heat efficient as are the closed-cell type of pads. For snow or extremely cold conditions, use a 2" thickness of the most dense foam available, and cover with hermopholyte. Two foam pads, one under the other, with a minimum of ½"thickness, will be very comfortable in most weather conditions, especially when you use Velcro tape to connect them to both sides of the sleeping bag so that they will move as you do. If possible, get a removable waterproof cover so that your pad may be used in many ways. An air mattress is only good for cushioning, and should only be used exclusively for short weekend trips due to its heavy pad weight. To increase an air mattress' effectiveness, you can stuff with feathers and get a type that will self-inflate.

How to Keep Warm at Night
1. Put on dry, warmed-up clothing (from the skin out) before going to sleep.

2. Keep head covered with a knitted stocking cap and breathe outside your bag. Don't pull your head inside of the bag which will cause the air to freeze up around the bag's opening and keeps your body moisture inside.

3. Put on dry wool stockings and or booties, and warm the foot of the bag with a hot rock wrapped in layers of paper or towel.

4. Eat a supper high in fats and do something to warm up

before going to bed. Don't sit or lie on cold ground, which. draws out your inner body heat. When air is very cold, preheat it by breathing through a scarf.

BACKPACKS

The characteristics which you need to consider when choosing a backpack are pack construction, capacity requirements, terrain use, frame size and weight, comfort, and desired range of expense, (you will be paying the most for quality and convenience). A reliable backpack needs to have good, stiff shoulder pads, no cracks in the wells, tightened pins, repaired straps, an adjustable, padded hip strap with a quick release buckle for safety, and be strong with straight, even stitching. The padded waist belt keeps the load stable and comfortable. You also need to have water-proof rain flaps over all compartments and zippers for protection from the elements. The larger size packs should be divided into smaller units to facilitate finding things easily and quickly. (See Fig. 4.3) Variations in packs include H- or U-shaped frame outlines, external or internal frame type, regular or "suspender" harness, back or top opening to main compartment, and small rucksack or any size up to the larger Everest-style pack. A good quality frame that fits your back properly is of much more importance than the kind of pack bag you select. Usually you should rent a couple of different types before deciding which one to purchase. Never buy a new pack without first testing it when loaded and adjusted to your back according to directions. Your pack should carry the load over the shoulders so that you can stand up straight, and not force you to waste energy by leaning forward to balance a poor load. (It also should not sit too low on the back in order to reduce fatigue.) (See Fig. 4.4) In addition to comfort, you should aim for the greatest capacity for the less amount of mass, and still have it maintain a high degree of maneuverability. Select all equipment so that you can backpack in for a week with only 30 pounds. A man and wife team can usually go on a weekend trip for under 30 pounds, and for a trip under nine days. Individual pack weight should never exceed 20% or 1/5 of each person's body weight. In rough and stormy wilderness, it may be necessary to have a load up to 40-50 pounds in order to insure a comfortable and weatherproof camp.

To be any good, a frame has to fit.

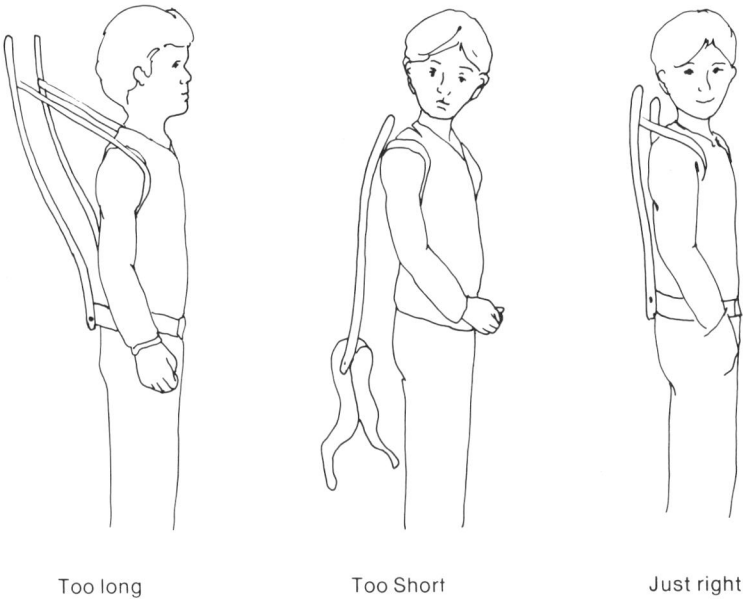

| Too long | Too Short | Just right |

Fig. 4.3 The Pack Frame

HOW TO PACK

A general guideline is to pack complimentary or similar items together in plastic bags to keep them dry and easy to locate. (See Fig. 4.5) Distribute the pack weight so that there is a soft surface against your back and light things are placed high and close to you. Keep trail, emergency gear, and rain clothing on top for easy accessibility, and always put gear back in the same location so that you'll know where to find it. You can usually lash all sleeping gear to the bottom of the pack with canvas straps, but don't use elastic

HOW TO PACK

Here's one suggested way to organize your equipment. Just combine things if your backpack has fewer compartments. Remember to carry a knife, waterproof matches, and compass on your person at all times.

FLAP POCKET

Fire & Camping Permits
Pencil & Paper
Identification of medical
restrictions & allergies

Fishing lines
Watch (if not worn)
Maps

BACK POCKET

Metal or plastic cups
Waterproof matches
Firestarter
Sunglasses
Lunch & trail snacks
Backpacking Handbook
Repair Kit
Scripture, paperback, etc.

Other licenses
Binoculars (if used)
Magnifying Glass (if used)
Camera
Windmeter, pocket
    thermometer
Day Pack
(Can put flashlight here)

UPPER LEFT POCKET

Flashlight plus spare
bulb and batteries or
second 1-quart canteen

UPPER RIGHT POCKET

1-quart canteen

UPPER COMPARTMENT

Rainware (Storm Shelter)
Sweatshirt
Personal Utensils
Cook kit or individual plate,
    cup & bowl
Stirring Spoon
Can opener
Hot mitten

1-burner Stove
Grill or Grate (if used)
Salt & Pepper with shaker
Wire coathanger
Food Containers
Sufficient food (plus extra)
Rubber bands
Extra plastic bags

LOWER LEFT POCKET	LOWER RIGHT POCKET
Toilet Articles	First Aid Kit
Toothbrush	2 Dimes
Toothpaste	Chapstick
Soap and towel	Repellent
Toilet paper	Sunburn Ointment
Paper Towels	Signal Whistle
Comb, brush	Matches in waterproof case
Wash'n' dries, etc.	Needle and thread
Scouring pad	Safety pins
Matches for cooking	Water Purification Tablets
Dish soap	Special Medicine
Foil	Salt Tablets
Other small cooking items	Moleskin
	Supplies for wounds, etc.

LOWER COMPARTMENT

Tent or Tube Tents
Tarp and Ground cloth (Rainfly)
Foam Pad (or air mattress)
50 feet of nylon cord
Appropriate clothing (plus extra)
    Stocking cap
    Wind breaker (loose layer system)
Recreation Equipment (if used)
    Fishing Tackle
    Watercolor Pad and Paints
    Nature books
    Games, etc.
    Shovel (if used)

STUFF BAG

Sleeping Bag
Small pillow or other sleeping items (if used)

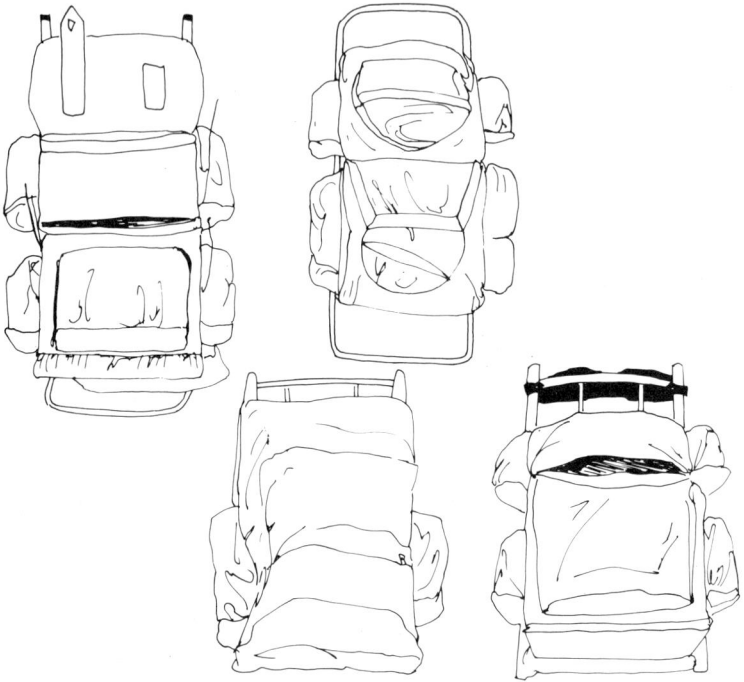

Representative packbags. Above left: two-thirds-length bag, divided. Main compartment top-opening with hold-open frame, lower compartment zippered. Above right: two-thirds-length bag, undivided, top-opening with drawstring closure. Below left: two-thirds-length bag, divided, back-opening with compression straps. Below right: full-length bag, divided, sleeping bag stowed in lower compartment.

Fig. 4.4 Types of packs

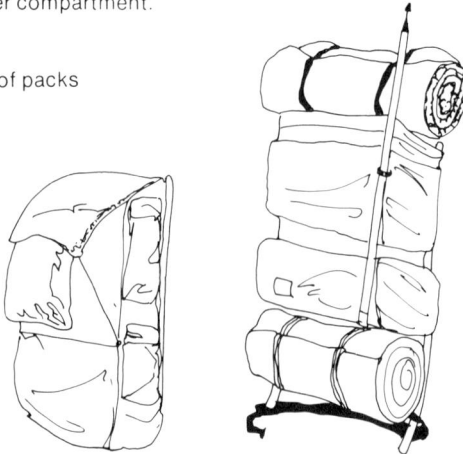

Representative packbags for very bulky loads. Left: full-length, undivided "expedition" bag. Gear also can be carried under the top flap. Right: two-thirds-length bag with entension frame (hidden) added for top load, exterior attachment points for lashing on gear.

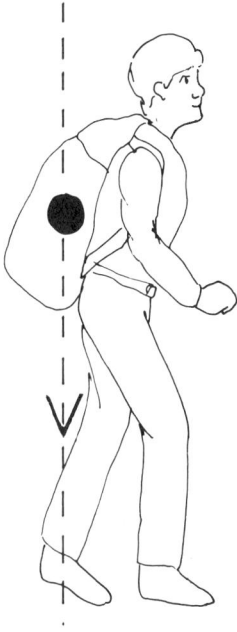

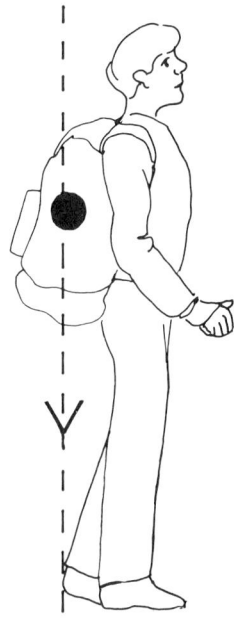

Fig. 4.5 How to Pack

shock cords. When trying to pack light, remember that eight, 1-ounce gadgets add up to 1/2 pound. Make the load as compact as possible, filling in all empty spaces with small, flexible or fragile items, and perhaps even put sleeping things in with the sleeping bag. Allow two pounds for each quart of water including its container. If necessary, you can make a "home made pack" by rolling items into your bag and tying it into a circle. To prevent broken frames and split bag seams, never drop your pack.

Hoisting the Loaded Pack

1. Grab it by the shoulder straps and lift to the knee, slip one arm through a strap, swing the load out, and slip in the other arm; or,
2. with pack on the ground, sit against it, slip on the straps, turn onto your knees and stand up. To get out of the pack, reverse the process.

When the load is heavy, use method two during rest stops. During brief breaks, rest the pack on a boulder or log while it is still on your back. (See Fig. 4.6)

Fig. 4.6 How to put on a heavy pack

5 Campsites & Shelters

CAMPSITE SELECTION ON THE TRAIL

There is no such thing as a "perfect" campsite for everyone. Different people desire different settings (such as a lake versus a stream, privacy versus people, etc.). Always set up camp before dark so that you may be aware of your surroundings.

Consider the following safety factors when selecting your "ideal spot":

1. **Protection from wind and storms** — set your tent up with its tail to the wind and with favorable exposure to the forenoon sun, and shade during the afternoon. During winter, try and camp in a place protected from icy blasts and driving snow (such as in a hollow, dense forest).

2. **Protection from natural disasters** — stay away from bodies of water and gullys to avoid flash floods and high tides, from overhanging cliffs to avoid rockfalls, from tinder dry forests during drought conditions to avoid fire traps, and from under large trees and dead branches to avoid danger from lightning.

3. **Protection from dangerous life** — choose an area free from poisonous plants (poison oak and ivy), insect pests (stay away from tall grass, swamps, heavy underbrush, or within thirty feet of water's edge to avoid mosquitos, midges, and black flies), and harmful animals (snakes, bears, etc.).

4. **Sufficient and safe drinking water** — always check the purity of your supply. Also consider a legal source of fire wood if needed for extra heat or light.

5. **Level and dry ground for bed** — keep away from creek bottoms, marsh, claysoil, and green grassy areas. Aim for a high and dry area, such as a level knoll on a gentle slope with gravel type soil, covered with tough grass turf. Stay fifteen feet above water level in order to get any cooling breezes, while avoiding fog and heavy dew.

In addition to safety, consideration of your surroundings must be included. Each backpacker needs to have an "ecological conscience" which will warn him when his presence is very harmful or distruptive to a specific area, and will help him select a campsite that will handle his amount of "impact", without resulting in a lasting "imprint" upon the spot of beauty he wishes to enjoy and not scar for someone else.

BACKPACKING TENTS

The variables to consider when selecting a tent are:

1. **Construction** — This includes the materials used, the tent layout, and where it is reinforced. Nylon taffeta or ripstop nylon is best for backpacking tents.

2. **Overall usage and location** — Determines how heavy and what quality of tent is necessary for your needs.

3. **Number of people** — Allow approximately 32 sq. ft. or 4' x 8' for each person's sleeping area.

4. **Weatherproof** — General resistance to weather and especially consider if it is waterproof.

5. **Weight** — Never carry more than 4 pounds per person for total shelter.

6. **Expense** — Goes along with the quality desired, although try not to buy any more than is required for your use. Quality companies include Camp Trails, Gerry, Kelty, R.E.I., and Cannondale.

A good backpack tent will allow for cross ventilation, with windows being covered from the inside. All points of stress, especially the ridge and the corners, should have reinforcement strips. Every seam should have four thicknesses, and grommets or peg loops should be sturdy. A quality tent will come with a rain fly, guylines, aluminum pole and pegs, and can weigh less than 2½ pounds per person. The rainfly solves the condensation problem involved when the tent gets wet inside. The inner layer of the tent is usually a type of breathable nylon, and the outer layer is made of plastic coated nylon. This double layer system allows the tent fabric to warm up and cause the moisture inside to escape to the outer layer. (An adult expels around 1½ pints of water overnight when asleep.) This system also keeps the rain entirely off of the tent itself. (See Fig. 5.0)

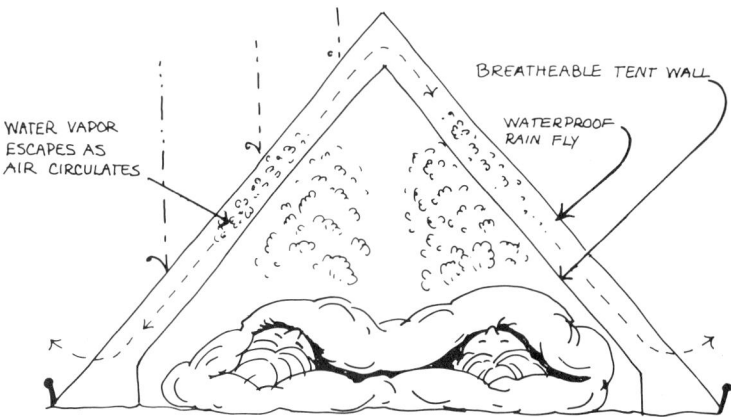

BREATHEABLE TENT WALL

WATERPROOF RAIN FLY

WATER VAPOR ESCAPES AS AIR CIRCULATES

Fig. 5.0 Breathing in the Rain

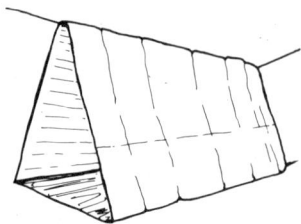

The tube tent, a dubious choice for the backpacker.

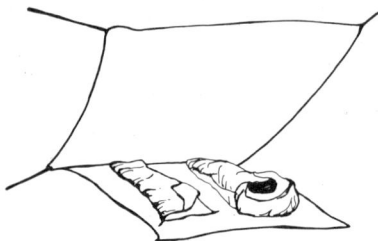

Polyethylene tarp (4-mil, tran-slucent) rigged as shed roof, adequate protection against gentle rains, radiating heat loss, and glaring sun.

Nylon tarp with built-in grommets, quickly and easily rigged as A-tent by use of two aluminum poles and eight lightweight pegs.

The most universal regular trail shelter, the backpack standard. Protection and comfort for two hikers in most circumstances.

The best and most expensive of the standard shelter designs is the expedition tent, required for long-term camping at high altitudes and in bitter cold. Many have frost liners, cooking facilities inside, and special safety features.

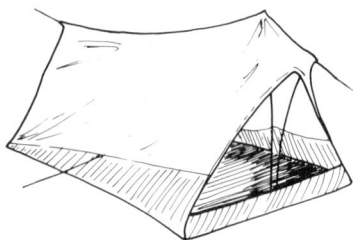

The modified tube is actually more of a backpack tent than a tube, suitable for at least summer hiking.

Fig. 5.1 Trailside shelters

The tent floor should be of plastic coated nylon, and is sewn in all around, preferably above the ground level. Doors and windows should zip completely shut and be protected by mosquito netting. It is convenient if they also can open from the top on down, in order to let the warm moist air that accumulates at the top pass out freely.

The advantages of having a tent are that it:(1) reduces radiation heat loss, (2) provides shade from the sun, (3) conserves body heat (it can be almost 10° F warmer inside a tent than the outer air temperature, and even more if windy), (4) allows for privacy from other campers, (5) helps protect from creatures and insects, and (6) provides wind and wet weather protection. In addition to keeping it as clean as possible, the best way to preserve your tent is to keep it away from any source of spark, and to resist the temptation to cook inside. (See Fig. 5.1)

The types of tents available include the standard one-pole tent, the A-frame, the crossridge or horizontal ridge line, and the self-supporting mountain tent (which is mainly for violent wind and weather conditions). These are what might be called "true tents." Possible substitutions include the single-layer tarp or tube tent which may be opened at both ends or have one end closed, have built-in grommets, and is best constructed of waterproof (polymer-coated) nylon. This type of a "tent" usually pitches by stringing it between two trees, can weigh less than one pound per person, and may have nylon netting for insect protection. A plain tarp made of Visqueen or polyethylene that is 2½' x 6', and is 4 mil. thick, put up with a nylon cord, may serve as a temporary shelter for one person. It will protect from vertically falling rain, heat loss and dew accumulation to a certain extent, is lightweight and inexpensive, and may easily be repaired with 2 inch cloth tape that has an adhesive backing.

(See Fig. 5.2)   **HOW TO PITCH A TENT**

Usually the best approach to putting up a tent is to follow all the instructions that are enclosed. However, if no guidelines are included, then these general steps may be followed:

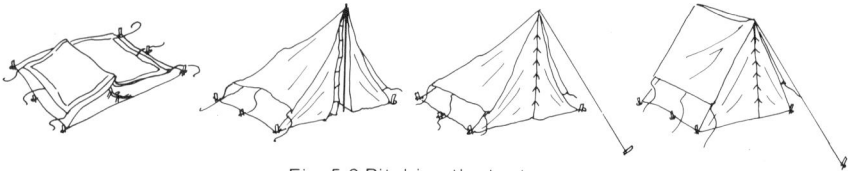

Fig. 5.2 Pitching the tent

1. Close door flaps. Peg down four corners at right angles.
2. Assemble front tent pole. Put in place.
3. Push down peg for front guy line and attach line.
4. Assemble rear tent pole, put in place. Attach rear guy line to peg and pull the ridge taut.
5. Push pegs into ground for four corner lines and for eave lines. Tighten lines to make roof smooth.
6. Push in remaining pegs. Open door flaps. Enter tent and spread sod cloth out flat all the way around.

Note that all line pulls start from center of tent.

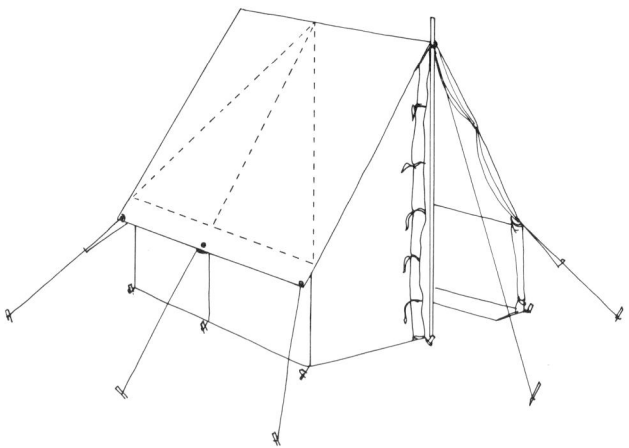

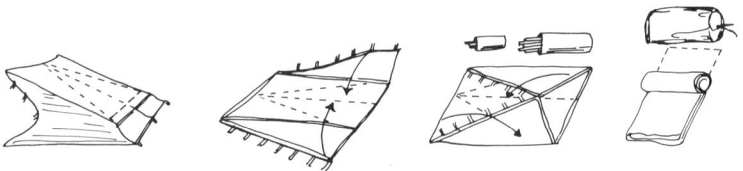

Fig. 5.3 Striking the tent

1. To strike tent, close door, loosen lines and pull out all pegs. Lay tent down flat.
2. Fold door flaps to middle of tent. Tuck in all lines.
3. Fold top and bottom over. Fold further to size of tent bag.
4. Roll up pole and peg bags in tent. Put tent in bag.

82

1. Select a level area and remove all prominent objects from the proposed tent area. Place tent floor on the ground with the door facing the leeward side (away from the wind). Close the door and window flaps and peg down the four corners at right angles to each other.

2. Assemble the front tent pole (unless it's a single aluminum pole) and put it in place, making the tent erect.

3. Hammer down the peg for the front guyline and attach the line.

4. Assemble the rear tent pole and put it in place. Attach the rear guyline to its peg and pull the ridge taunt.

5. Hammer in the pegs for the four corner lines and for eavelines. Tighten all lines to make the tent roof smooth.

6. Hammer in all of the remaining pegs and open the door flaps to air out. Enter the tent and spread a sod or ground cloth out to protect the tent floor.

Another alternative is to pitch your tent between two trees, using the trunks or strong branches instead of the front and rear guyline pegs. You may even be able to get away with not bringing poles, if you can tighten and tie all lines so that there is no slack in the tent roof. Always make sure a tent is sun-dried and swept clean before folding it up to prevent mildew, unnecessary deterioration, etc.

To Strike A Tent (See Fig. 5.3)
1. Close the door and window, loosen lines and pull out all pegs and poles. Lay the tent down flat.

2. Fold door flaps to the middle of tent and tuck in all lines.

3. Fold the top and bottom over and keep folding until it will fit into the tent bag.

4. Roll up the pole and peg bags inside the tent and put everything into the carrying bag.

Always check and tighten the tent lines from time to time, except during rainy weather, when you should slacken the lines to offset shrinking of wet lines and tent material. Lines should be kept taut using a tent-cord tightener of nylon or aluminum (also called slides, slips, or runners). This helps you to tighten slacking lines by adjusting only the slide, and not having to relocate the peg. Lightweight slides are made from aluminum, plywood, or dowel sticks. Pegs can be made of wood, steel, or rod aluminum (which holds well except in rocky ground). They can be made at home out of scrap wood, dowel sticks, aluminum corner molding, branches, plywood, etc. You'll need high-impact plastic pegs for a gravel or beach (sand) surface. Lightweight tent pegs are usually set at a 90° angle, although this may vary with the type of ground and the kind of peg that is used. Never "ditch" a tent to control run-off except when absolutely necessary.

ON-SITE SHELTERS

For those emergency situations when you are surprized by a sudden rainstorm, or other extenuating circumstances, which somehow prevent pitching of your tent, a temporary on site shelter will have to do. You may take cover under an overhanging cliff or beneath a thickly bowed tree against the wind and where the break is needed. However, these types of shelters should not be relied upon for very long and hikers should always be on guard for lightning or any potential rockslides which might endanger him. Also, never cut off branches from trees or makes any permanent marks on the land in order to build a shelter or exercise woodcraft skills.

6 Cooking & Food

MENU PLANNING

When you are selecting the food to take on your outing, there are a few important factors which you need to be aware of. For short term trips, it is not essential to be too careful about the kind of food you take as long as it is sufficient for your needs and will keep you from feeling any hunger pains. However in planning for longer trips, you will need to check the amount of calories and grams of protein contained in the food for each day of your proposed menu. A simple "calorie-counter" found in most sporting goods or department stores is very useful and it helps you to approximate the caloric intake that you want for your trip. Especially during winter outings, you'll need a lot of calories contained within heat stimulating foods that provide a great deal of energy for body warmth and activities. A minimum of 9 to 15 ounces of something warm (which contain a supply of carbohydrates) is best for breakfast on a cold winter's day. It is also essential to plan for a menu full of energy foods and a source of vitamin C. Another guideline here is to plan for about 1½ pounds (dry weight) of food per day. The wise backpacker will plan for well balanced, appetizing meals in addition to being sufficient in calories and grams of protein. The types of food that can fulfill these requirements are (1) regular supplies from your kitchen shelf, (2) freeze-dried, which is most often packed in a plastic serving pouch or tray (and weighs 90 percent less without the H_2O than home cooked food), and (3) powdered or dehydrated (allow 1½ to 2 pounds per day if all your food is dehydrated). Make sure that whatever foods you decide upon can be easily prepared with a minimum amount of equipment. Also try and avoid any potential leftovers but pack in enough energy food for two meals.

One hint for meat dishes is not to plan on eating fish because you won't end up eating if the fish don't bite. In other words, as far as food is concerned, plan to fill all your nutritional needs from the supplies that you bring. Also, it is very convenient if you can buy alot of small packets of food although this is less economical Mountain shops stock many kinds of plastic (mainly polyethylene) bags, bottles, and jars for hauling foods, including water. Strong, light transparent poly bags, in sizes from 5-by-8 to 15-by-18 inches, costing from 1-10¢ each, have many uses.

Table 1
General Calorie and Protein Guide

Age	Male		Female	
11-14 yrs	2800 calories	(44 grams)	2400 calories	(44 grams)
15-18 yrs	3000 calories	(54 grams)	2100 calories	(48 grams)
22 yrs	3000 calories	(54 grams)	2100 calories	(46 grams)
45 yrs	2700 calories	(56 grams)	2060 calories	(46 grams)
65 yrs	2400 calories	(56 grams)	1800 calories	(46 grams)

Lunch

Under most trip conditions, the lunch should be simple, easy and quick to prepare and should fit in with other planned activities for that day. When you plan to spend the day in camp, a freeze-dried meal might be desirable, while a much simpler meal such as sandwiches and fruit would be better for a lunch which is to be eaten on the trail during or on an afternoon hike.

An increasing variety of dehydrated and freeze dried foods, often called "dried," "instant," or "minute foods," can be found on the shelves of your local supermarket. They are usually cheaper than those purchased from specialized suppliers. If you are planning substantial purchases, ask the manager to help you find what he has available. You will also find suitable foods at Oriental and health food stores. Here are some possibilities:

Bread, biscuit, muffin, cornbread, and pancake mixes
Cake, cookie, brownie, and gingerbread mixes
Oatmeal, grits, cornmeal, farina, Granola, Grapenuts
Dried peas, lentils, and beans of all types
Instant rice
Skillet dinners
Dried soups
Dried fruits (apricots, raisins, apples, prunes, dates, figs, fruit cocktail)
Macaroni, spaghetti, noodles, pizza
Hard cheese
Pream and other non-dairy products
Instant pudding, Jello (cool in a stream)
Dried milk (a pound makes a gallon of milk) — this is usually skim milk, but dried whole milk is available
Instant potatoes
Powdered fruit juices
Parsley, onion, and carrot flakes
Instant cocoa, coffee and tea, malted milk tablets, Ovaltine
Popcorn (excellent for campfire nibbling)
Peanuts and other nuts, hard candy, and non-melting chocolate
Dried beef, codfish flakes and cakes
Pemmican (dried meat pounded to a pulp and then mashed with fat and sometimes raisins and sugar and formed into cakes or bars)
Beef jerky (thin, brown strips that you can suck on)
Wilson bacon bar
Hard cookies, such as ginger snaps
Boullion cubes, dried mushrooms, and gravy mixes (excellent for adding flavor to soups and casseroles)
Pie and cobbler mixes
Herbs and spices — choose a few favorites, such as ground cummin, thyme, herb mixtures, cinnamon, cloves, bay leaves, dried dill, rosemary, and sage

Dinner

The backpacker's dinner should provide the biggest source of protein for the day, and the bulk of the required foods should be included here. It is advisable to plan the first night's meal so that it will be very easy to prepare since you will most likely be tired from just hiking. You may even bring fresh meat for that night if it is frozen and correctly packed and wrapped in layers of paper. Once again, you should be reminded that in the winter you will need to have a meal that is high in calories, protein, carbohydrates, and includes a lot of liquid.

TRAIL MEALS THAT DON'T NEED COOKING

There are foods that preferably don't spoil, melt, crumble, squish, and are nourishing, compact, and light to carry. In planning trail foods, consider the amount of available water. If water is limited do not include food that will create thirst. Examples include High-Energy-Snack-Foods with more carbohydrates, raisins, peanuts, chocolate candy, candy corn, M & M's, dried fruit, and gorp.

Backpackers' Superbars
½ C. butter or margarine
¾ C. brown sugar, packed
½ C. quick-cooking oats
½ C. unsifted whole wheat flour
½ C. unsifted all-purpose flour
¼ C. toasted wheat germ
2 tsp. grated orange rind
2 eggs
1 C. whole blanched almonds
¼ C. raisins
¼ C. flaked coconut
½ C. semi-sweet chocolate bits

1. In medium bowl of electric mixer, beat butter with ½ cup of the brown sugar until soft and blended.

2. At low speed beat in oats, whole wheat and all-purpose flours, wheat germ and orange rind. Pat into an ungreased 8 x 8 x 2-inch square pan.

3. Mix eggs, almonds, raisins, coconut, chocolate bits and remaining ¼ cup brown sugar; pour over the base and spread evenly.

4. Bake in preheated 350° F. oven about 30 to 35 minutes or until almonds are golden brown.

5. Cool, then cut into 12 bars or squares; wrap with plastic film to keep moist.

Makes 12 bars.

Breakfast Foods
Instant cereal, instant cocoa, dried fruits, powdered juice mix, Tang, and bacon bars.

Lunch Foods
Salami sticks, canned meat, beef jerky, cheese and crackers, nuts, biscuits, carrots, peanut butter, honey, jam, vegetable sticks, dried or dehydrated fruits, marshmallows, powdered juice, Kool-aid, and sandwiches.

Supper Foods
Fresh fruits, apples or oranges (to help quench thirst), vegetable sticks, carrots, celery, radishes, canned meats, instant pudding, hard cookies, and powdered milk.

Examples of Possible Menus
Sample Breakfast
Regular: dry cereal, famalia or add dried fruit to cereal with milk, Tang or orange drink, sugar, powdered milk, cocoa. You can make a cocoa mixture with powdered milk, sugar, and cinnamon at home, cornbread or gingerbread mix, and vegaline.

One Person: A. 1 cup pancake mix, ½ cup sugar or syrup, cocoa, powdered milk for pancakes and cocoa, two eggs, vegalene, and orange.

B. Freeze-dried hash browns, instant oatmeal, cheese omelet, orange beverage, egg with butter, cooking oil and cocoa.

Sample Lunch
Trail Lunch: tuna salad sandwich, orange, nuts, cookies or candy bar, cinnamon grahams, canteen with

water or fruit punch (the equivalent of 3, 12-ounce glasses of liquid)

Freeze-dried: beef almondine or vegetable and macaroni, cottage cheese or applesauce, banana pudding or cake mix, dried fruit.

Sample Dinners (all can be prepared at home before leaving)

Regular: (for first night out)

Foil dinner: hamburger or pattie spread with dry onion soup mix and butter, cubed potatoes, carrots, onions, salt and pepper, and 1 teaspoon water; wrapped in foil layers.

Baked apples (place apple in several layers of aluminum foil, core the center and peel ⅓ of the way down and fill with red hots, marshmallows, and brown sugar, cinnamon, butter, nuts, and raisins. Be sure to bring foil up and around the sides and twist at the top.

Baked fresh pineapple (should be wrapped in foil and cooked for 45 to 60 minutes until tender)

Shish-kabobs: this can consist of cubes of beef, onions, apples, tomatoes; steak, bacon and onions; eggplant, tomatoes, lamb, and onions; hamburger balls, onions, tomatoes, and green peppers; ham, apples and tomatoes; scallops, shrimp and bacon; or calves' liver, tomatoes, onions, mushrooms or cucumbers attached on a stick and cooked over the fire or wrapped in foil and roasted in the coals.

Canned hash (wrapped in double baggies) or canned chili and carrots and celery.

Freeze-dried: chicken noodle soup, beef stroganoff, punch, butterscotch pudding, beef stew, potato chowder, fruit cocktail, chocolate cream pie, lemonade.

COOKING TECHNIQUES

When discussing outdoor cooking techniques, you need to be aware of the many varieties of equipment which can be utilized in the preparation of a meal on the trail. This equipment can range anywhere from a very deluxe Butane two-burner stove, to a simplistic homemade Bunson-type burner. Outdoor cooking fires are a very common method of food preparation although they are most costly in terms of environmental damage and wasted energy. When all factors are considered, the backpacking stove is the most ecologically sound, fuel efficient, and easiest tool to use to cook your wilderness meal.

Backpacking Stoves

The advantages of a stove over a campfire are that it is easier, cleaner, and most importantly, it "leaves no trace." Selection of a stove mainly depends upon what kind of fuel you prefer, but whatever the type, you will always need to keep the fuel pure and the stove clean. Always be cautious around a backpacking stove, and it is a good idea to practice with a new one before leaving home.

Gasoline — This is the most volatile of all fuels and can easily explode. It is also called "white gas" and the safest type is the can brand name appliance gas (such as "Coleman") since it is filtered clean and stays volatile the longest. The best brands of this type of stove are the Optimus, Svea, Phoebus, and MSRQ. Always follow instructions carefully and use proper stove accessories such as an aluminum fuel bottle with a filter, a vented pouring spout, a cleaning wire and an eye dropper. (See Fig. 6.0)

Kerosene — Although having the same BTU (heating power) as white gas, kerosene is less volatile and flammable. It won't explode, and this type of stove also operates on stove or diesel oil. Optimus is the top-name make for this product. You will need to use a "fire ribbon" or some canned heat ("Sterno") to ignite it.

Butane — This type of stove is very popular because it is easy and quick to start, very dependable, and has been proven to be "tent safe." The fuel is liquified, low pressure petroleum gas, and comes in a thin metal cartridge which makes it convenient to carry and simple to adjust. Disadvantages are that it is heavier than gas or kerosene while more expensive, gives off less hot heat, doesn't freely vaporize below 32° F (which means it will not operate well in cold, high altitude and wind), and fumes often leak from the cartridge. Also, you can't tell how much fuel is left in a used cartridge, and will need to pack it out when empty. Reliable brands are EFI, Optimus, Gas, Primus, and Rich-Moor Alp. (Get the U.S., not the French makes).

RECOMMENDED STOVES FOR BACKPACKING

Figures may vary with different models — these are only averages of test results done in no wind and with a moderate temperature.

Fuel / STOVE	Capacity of Tank or Cartridge (Pints)	Approximate High-Flame Burning Time of one Tank or Cartridge	Approximate Time to Boil 1 quart water (Minutes at sea level)	*Weight without fuel @ Weight of full cartridge (pounds)	Approx. Cost *without fuel @ cost of one cartridge
White Gas (Svea and Optimus)	1/3-1/2 (one model is 1)	3/4-2½	6-8, 7-9 (one model is 3-5)	1-1/8-1-3/4* (one model is 3½*)	$15-$19* (one model is $30*)
Kerosene (Optimus)	1-1-3/4	2½-4	4-6, 5-7	1-5/8-2½*	$20*
Butane Gas or EFI	3/4	3	10-12	5/8@-7/8* (one model is ½*)	$10 $1@
Alcohol (Simple Burner)	1/3	1/2	8-10	1/4*	$3*
Propane	No Figures	No Figures	No Figures	No Figures	No Figures

Fig. 6.0 Recommended stoves for backpacking

Propane — This is also a form of liquified petroleum gas, with the main difference from butane being that it will vaporize down to -50° F. This means that it is excellent for cold weather, although it comes in heavy steel cylinders which are not practical for ordinary trips. Never throw a propane container into the fire — it will explode.

Alcohol — The simple burner alcohol stove has one-half the BTU rating of white gas and kerosene, is therefore slow cooking, and the fuel is very expensive. However, it does burn cleaner than the other fuels, leaves no soot, and is non-toxic and non-explosive. The most difficult problem is finding one, although the best bet is usually to look in a specialized mountain shop. (See Fig. 6.1)

The factors to consider when purchasing a stove are the weight of the stove, weight of the fuel, ease and convenience of use, cost of stove, cost of fuel, and safety. For long multi-day trips, the amount of fuel consumption and heat output will become especially important. Beginning packers usually start with butane stoves, but as they extend their camping to colder conditions, end up preferring the gas or kerosene. Always carry plenty of fuel and double any theoretical figures which are given for cooking time.

OTHER TYPES OF STOVES

There are many alternatives to your brand name type backpacking stoves which will also cook your food easily and will not take a toll on nature and beauty. A very simple and inexpensive tin can stove can be made with a unit of "sterno canned heat" and a two pound metal can which has been punctured six to eight times around the bottom edge and three to four times around the top. Sterno is pink solidified, ethyl alcohol which is almost completely smokeless, odorless, and provides an excellent source of hot heat. It is very safe, lights instantly, burns at 1650° F. at the top of the flame and will start fires in the snow or rain. One can of sterno (7 ounces) will burn for about two hours, long enough to cook several meals. Also, when properly utilized, less than eight ounces of sterno will cook two large meals, sufficient for at least three adults. (See Fig. 6.2)

One alternative to sterno fuel is that of commercial tablets which are one inch in diameter and only a half-inch

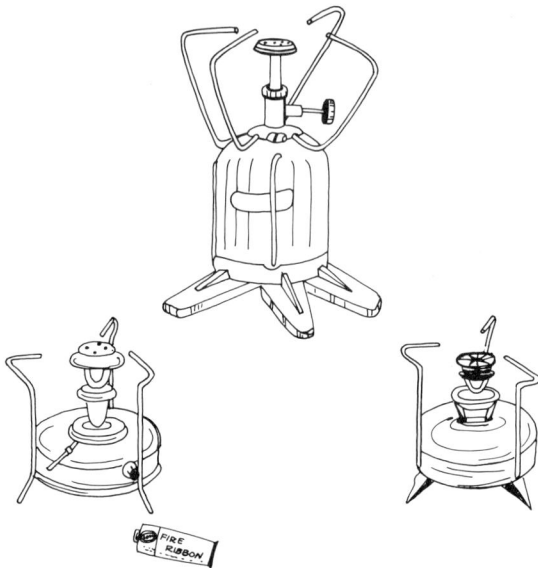

Popular kerosene stoves. Left: Optimus 48. Right: Optimus 00. Burner plates available for both. Front: fire ribbon for priming.

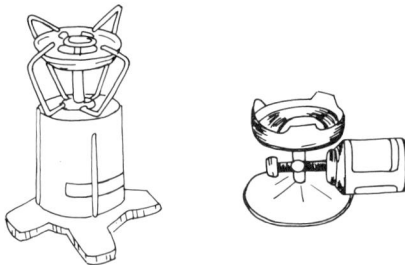

Popular butane stoves, with cartridges in place. Left: Gaz S-200 (vapor feed). Right: EFI Mini-stove, marketed under many brand names (liquid feed).

Stove accessories: aluminum fuel bottle, plastic funnel, and pouring spout for the bottle.

Fig. 6.1 Popular stoves

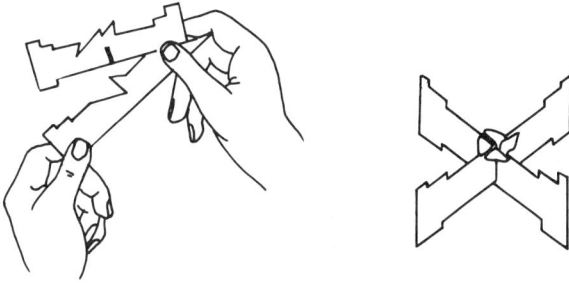

This "25¢ stove" is as practical and foolproof as it is inexpensive. The cross-bars keep the cooking container at the correct height over the burning fuel. They also act as a flue to guide flame and heat upward, thus adding to efficiency. Without doubt this is the lowest cost, smallest, most reliable and most sensible little stove ever invented.

With a little outfit like this, cooking dehydrated or freeze-dried foods is easy, so many tasty menus can be planned for outings and everything can be carried with minimum bulk and weight. While the little stove can cook only one thing at a time, it will cook enough of it for several people. Thus, one person can cook one kind of food on his stove and another person can prepare something else on theirs.

Fig. 6.2 Sterno Kit

thick. They can be placed in a small stove or lighted inside of different sized cooking cans. In addition to the tin can stove there are the single and double burner cook stoves which are only 6½ inches by 13½ inches and are half-inch wide when folded. The lowest cost, smallest, and most reliable type of stove is the home-made "cross bars." It is made simply by fitting a small grill over the top of a can of liquid heat. It will only be four inches by 1½ inches in size and weigh less than two ounces.

Even though it is always easiest to use some type of backpacking stove rather than an open fire, you should be sure to be prepared to use one when it rains, when a wood fire is unsafe, or when an area has been devastated by too much wood gathering and fire building. If you must light an open fire, remember that a small fire is more efficient for cooking than a large one and follow all of the fire safety regulations. Also, if necessary during wet weather you can keep your fuel dry overnight by building your fire and then cover with a plastic bag.

Cooking Gear (see equipment list)

You may choose to use a simple Boy Scout mess kit or many go all out by purchasing a six man cooking set. But whatever your choice, keep it lightweight and practical. If you want to use any kind of a deep well cooker, get an aluminum, easily packed kind of model and remember that it is used most efficiently when the heat is concentrated around the bottom and the sides of the pot. The cooker requires a lid to keep the heat and moisture inside and conserve your heat so that it goes into the cooking pot and is not just blown away. If necessary, do your cooking inside the tent, out of the wind with your stove but be aware of fire danger. Handy items to include beside your pans and eating utensils are a spatula, tongs, mitten, large long-handled stirring spoon and plenty of foil and paper towels. (See Fig. 6.3)

Food Preparation

There are many handy tips and shortcuts for the preparation of food in the outdoors. There are entire books which have been written about this subject such as Dian Thomas' **Roughing It Easy**. Therefore, in recognition of the many useful and valuable treatises which are now available,

Scout cook kit — single camper

Trailchef cook kit — 10-16 people

Mountain cookset — 2 to 5 people

Fig. 6.3 Cooking kits

we will only mention a few of the more basic and convenient of these numerous cooking hints. Some foods act as natural buffers against the heat while giving the foods inside additional flavor. Some examples of this cooking technique are (a) egg or meat cooked inside an onion; (b) cake or muffin mix cooked inside an orange; (c) an orange, marshmallow, and chocolate cooked inside a banana. Also, you can heat liquids such as water or milk in a paper cup or sack and they will not burn the container as long as there is still some liquid inside. You can cook hardboiled eggs this way or just fry up bacon and egg breakfasts on a hot rock which has previously been heated in the coals. To preserve bacon longer, wash it off with a clean cloth using vinegar instead of water. Save the bacon grease for flavoring other foods such as beans and eggs. You can make pioneer roasting corn while the corn is still in the husk, by gently pulling back the husks and cleaning off the silk, butter and salt the inside, replace the husk, tie the ends and secure. Wrap the corn in foil or hot newspaper and bake in the coals or prop upright at the side of the fire until done. This kind of foil cooking can also be done with potatoes.

Freeze dried foods are very handy and easily prepared, although they are quite expensive compared to foods from your kitchen shelf. If you buy freeze dried meat, first soak in water and then cook like fresh meat. It will usually serve two to four people. Rules for the general preparation of freeze dried foods are (1) open the package and add boiling water; (2) stir and wait five minutes (longer if you're in a higher altitude), (3) eat right from the package or on a plate. Some helpful tips are when the directions call for hot water, use boiling water, and when cold water, the colder the better. Rip the foil package down the center and leave the inner plastic bag inside. The foil helps keep the food warm while rehydrating and gives strength to the plastic bag. You will then only need something to boil the water in since you can eat out of the package. You should always try to mix, cook and serve things in the easiest way possible. Mix items in a plastic bag, and then cook them in a can or in a foil-lined pan. It is also convenient to serve your meal in a foil bowl or a foil-lined mess kit. Soap the outside of any pans you intend to use before putting them over a fire or stove, with liquid detergents or soap for easier cleanup. You can use paper towels to wipe the dishes and get the grease out of the pan before washing them with water. It's wise to put your diswater on to heat before you start to eat the meal so that it will be all ready for use when you finish.

FOOD HANDLING AND STORAGE

When packing food for a backpack trip, you need to repackage all dry foods into sealed plastic bags, like baggies or ziplocks. Also, repackage all glass and canned items in secure plastic containers. Label everything you intend to use for each meal with the name of the item, the enclosed quantity and clear instructions for its preparation. Include which meal it is to be served in, what day it is planned for and put all the items for one meal together in a lunch sized paper sack or large plastic bag. An example of this labeling system is

Friday Dinner
1 pkg of (3) macroni & beef dinner
Carrots, cake mix
Kool-aid   Serves 4

You can use a gerryplastic tube for carrying butter, peanut butter, jelly, etc. in a neat efficient way. Carry eggs in a plastic egg container or place them in the cup inside of a mess kit and secure.

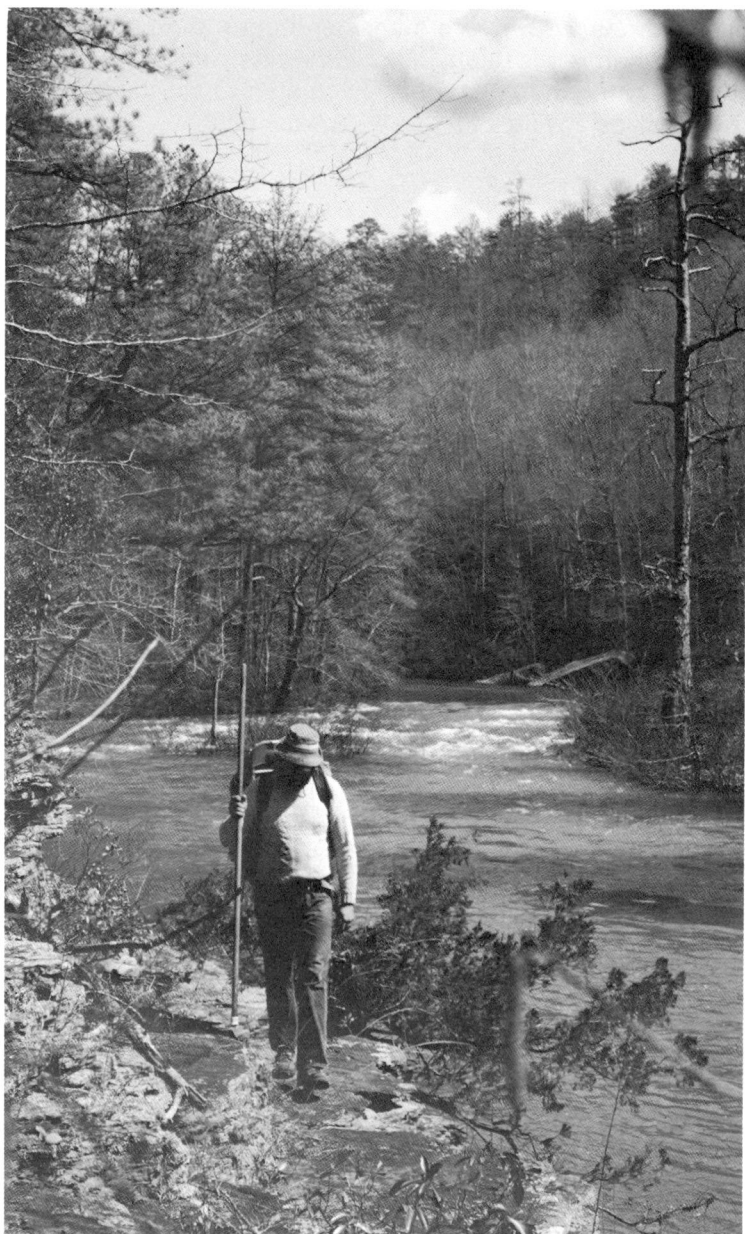

7 General Guidelines & Cautions

SAFETY

1. Always be prepared for the worst possible conditions, "Mother Nature has no respect for the unprepared." Never take unnecessary chances; if you become ill, get closer to civilization and a lower elevation as quickly as possible. Be aware of wild animals in your area of travel and leave them alone.

2. "Leave No Trace" and be conservation minded. (See Firebuilding and Hiking Sections). Camp one hundred feet away from lakes and streams and don't pollute, wash away from water's edge, don't carve or deface trees or shrubs, kill or harm nothing that you do not plan to eat and take only pictures, leave only footprints. Dispose of all garbage, (anything that can't be totally burned should be carried out — foil takes 32 years to decompose, plastic takes 200 years), destroy all evidence of your camp so that no one can tell you were there, and pick up other's litter (ask people on the way out if you can take out any trash for them).

Do your homework. Experienced backpackers do some research before they leave. You'll want to know about anything that would make your trip less pleasant so take the time and trouble to learn something about the area you will be visiting. Are the mosquitos bad in summer? Are there poisonous snakes? What kind of animals roam the woods? Is there a danger of rock slides or floods? Get some maps and any brochures available. If you're backpacking in a state or national park, get a copy of the regulations.

Tell someone where you're going. Just as important as your own preparation, is letting someone know where you're going and when you expect to be back. This is especially important as people will know where to look if you don't get back as expected.

Know your own limits. Strenuous exercise and extremes of temperature or altitude can be dangerous if you're not accustomed to such exercise. It's also important to recognize your own fears. Do heights make you nervous? Do you chill or tire easily? Don't be tempted to take on a situation that looks even a little threatening to you.

Keep your distance from wild animals. Even the cutest little chipmunk in the woods can be dangerous. In the woods, diseases like rabies, pneumonic plague (bubonic plague in humans) are so common among wildlife that there's no way to eradicate them. Skunks are especially susceptible to packing these diseases so admire the animals; don't try to pet them.

3. Be considerate of other backpackers — let people sleep, avoid loud noise and boisterous conduct, carry your share of food and equipment, don't move or damage trail signs, keep dogs on leash, etc.

Possible Ideas for Groups — Relays — packing or backpack, team competitions (tent pitching, best trail or cooked meal, etc.) trail rallys, and progressive lunch hikes.

Special Terms
Day Pack — Pouches that fasten to a belt with loops, or strap around waist to supplement pockets. Usually made of nylon or cotton with 1-2 outside pockets and shoulder straps.

Guy Line — Refers to any rope that maintains an upright structure. Used to sustain tent roof and walls.

Poncho — A nylon or plastic sheet, blanket, etc. Slit in the center so that the wearer can have the covering rest on his shoulders while sheltering his body, with his head through the slit. Designed to be used for protection while walking and resembles a portable tent.

Rucksack — A small, frameless bag that is usually used to carry loads for full-day or overnight outings only. There are internal, flexible frame models or "soft packs" for trips lasting up to a week.

Wilderness — Areas in a National Forest or Park where no wheeled vehicles of any kind are permitted. They can be reached only by foot, canoe, or horseback and contain no improved or "modern" facilities.

FIRST AID AND EMERGENCY CARE

Whether backpacking alone or with a group, every backpacker should carry with him a personal first aid kit. This unit will contain all of the things which are listed under the category of "One-Day Trip," and may be supplemented by a "Family Kit" or by items distributed among other members of your group. However, certain items must be carried by each person and kits should be carried with you on all outings away from camp. You need to keep your kit fastened or tied to a belt, or in an accessible place in your pack (such as the lower right hand pocket). Keep all medicine fresh and clearly marked, and make sure your kit is always up-to-date. When packing tablets or pills together in the same container, make sure they are separated or labeled so that you know what you are taking. You can get ready prepared (See table of First Aid Supplies) first aid kits at most mountaineering shops, although they are usually quite expensive considering what is included.

EMERGENCY NEEDS

Most of the injuries that occur to backpackers are minor and as common as those that happen around the house but because backpacking means being out of reach of a telephone or miles from the nearest hospital knowing what to do in an emergency is vital. You need a personal first aid kit. The kit itself should include bandage strips, sterile gauze pads, adhesive tape, and gauze bandages. You'll need some cotton balls, liquid soap, alcohol and premoistened

FIRST AID AND EMERGENCY SUPPLIES

All items under "1-day trip" should be carried in belt kit (bandaid box tied to belt with scarf or snap-on Army bag)

ITEM	1-Day Trip	Over-Night Trip	2-Day Plus Trip	Dist. Among Group	COMMENTS/OPTIONAL	SUBSTITUTION(S)
Emergecy dimes*	X	X	X		For phone calls-can tape to the inside of lid of bandaid box or other container.	
Special medicine	X (opt)	X	X		Depends on individual needs. Includes extra prescriptions for allergies, diabetes, etc.	
Eyeglasses	X (opt)	X (opt)	X		Extra pair or contacts and cleaning/wetting solution.	
Salt tablets*	X	X	X	X (extra)	12-24 enteric coated pills, to prevent or treat heat exhaustion, for fatigue and cramps. Need winter supply to use.	Salt packets will work but not as handy or easy to take.
Bandaids*	C	X	X		4 to 6 of ¾" or 1" size — assorted. For small lacerations. "Butterfly" type too.	
Triangular bandage	X (opt)		X	X	Need 2 for a group — 37" x 37" x 52". For a large wound.	Can make from 40" cloth cut on bias, in emergency use a bandana.
Adhesive tape	X (opt)	X	X	X	1" or 2" roll for group — for holding bandages, covering blisters, taping ankles, not winter proof roll on cardboard and flatten.	
Gauze bandage	X (opt)	X (opt)	X	X	4 individually wrapped 3" x 3" or 2" x 2". For a group also 4 4" x 4". Each person carry some.	Layered squares of sterilized cloth — clean and absorbent.
Burn ointment			X	X	1 tube ⅓ - ½ oz size. Carry some per person. For burns, and sunburn (Foile, Amerton, 1st aid cream).	Submerge in cold water or ice to ease pain temporarily.
Sterile applicator sticks			X	X	Sting kill swabs with cotton tips to clean, or apply medication.	Qtips, sterile absorbent cotton balls, or sterile cloth.

Item					Description	Notes
Aspirin*	X	X	X	X (extra)	6-12 tablets, for pain and fever, carry some person. 1-2 every 4 hours. Watch allergies.	Tylenol if allergic to aspirin.
Anti-bacterial soap		X (opt)	X	X	Small piece of "Dial" or similar type. Keep wrapped in plastic, carry some per person.	Liquid soap, Wash 'N Dri's if nothing else.
Antihistamine			X	X	6 capsules or tablets for colds, allergic reactions to insect bites or hives; don't get sleepy.	
Disinfectant/Antiseptic		X (opt)	X	X	Powder or liquid, for cleaning minor wounds. Alcohol, Bactine, etc., Tincture of iodine.	
Tweezers		X (opt)	X	X	Sterilize first, for splinters, thorns, etc.	Sterilized needle.
Antacids	X		X	X	6 for nausea; over exertion and altitude. Tums, Rolaids, Gelusil, Amphogel.	Baking soda for indigestion relief.
Halazone tablets*	X	X	X	X (extra)	Carry some per person, depends on water supply (see water purification).	Other methods of purifying — iodine, boiling, etc.
Eyedrops		X	X	X	To clean eyes, clear redness, some per person (Visine)	
Butane lighter	X		X			
(Needle)	X	X	X	X	Medium-sized needle, already threaded needle for opening blisters, repairing clothes.	Can sew with dental floss — makes extra strong binding.
Ammonia	X		X	X	Packaged tightly, for fainting and insect bites. 3 tubes inhalent for group — carry some per person.	
Mineral oil			X	X	Carry some per person, packaged tightly. For ticks.	
Moleskin	X	X	X	X	For blisters, can be patches or pads that need to be cut out or mole foam.	Bandaids and tape not as good.
Safety pins	X	X	X		Minimum of six assorted sizes. Holds clothes and pack together, fixes zippers, etc.	
Razor blade		X (opt)	X	X	Single edged, shaves hairy spots before taping, minor surgery, cutting tape and moleskin.	Tape one side of double edge blade.

ITEM	1-Day Trip	Over-Night Trip	2-Day Plus Trip	Dist. Among Group	COMMENTS/OPTIONAL	SUBSTITUTION(S)
Throat lozenges			X	X	Optional. Six for minor sore throats.	Oral antiseptic; Listerine, Chloreseptic etc.
Small scissors			X	X	Optional — nice to have for cutting.	Pocket knife.
Holocaine HC1 eye ointment			X	X	1-1/6 oz. tube for snow blindness. Optional — small amount under eyes every four hours.	
Snakebite kit	X	X	X	X	Suction type — follow directions carefully. Optional.	Don't try to treat if close to medical help (See First Aid Section)
Boullion cubes			X		3 cubes — warms inner body. For salt, energy and emergency food source.	Tea packets.
Extra shoe laces			X		Hiking shoe size.	String.
Signal whistle*	X	X	X		Only for emergencies. 3 toots sends for help to show location.	3 of anything is S.O.S. signal.
Ace bandage			X	X	Two for group, for sprains, pressure on wounds, 3" wide. Optional.	Sterilized strips of cloth; clean and absorbent.
Gauze roll			X	X	For individual — 1, 2" roll; for group — 1, 3" and 1, 4" roll. For large cuts.	
First Aid/ Survival booklet	X (opt)	X (opt)	X	X	To help with diagnosis and treatment. Emergency manual, Red Cross booklet, Scout handbook, etc.	

towelettes, for cleaning or burns. Other essentials are scissors, a small thermometer, flashlight, needles (sterilized to remove splinters), tweezers, oil skins for blisters and a chemical ice pack.

The medication should include aspirin and drugs for diarrhea, nausea, and vomiting, heartburn, indigestion, constipation, as well as a decongestant for colds. Don't forget suntan lotion and a sunburn ointment, an ointment for insect bites and stings and mild burns and an antibiotic ointment available without prescription for cuts or abrasions that may become infected.

WATER PURIFICATION

You can purify your water supply by boiling water for 20 minutes and then adding two halazone, chlorine or globulin tablets, or one iodine tablet for every quart of clear water. If the water is dirty, murky or cloudy, double the strength of the purifying agent or add two drops of household bleach such as Clorox or Purex per quart to destroy any bacteria. Then boil for 40 minutes. Follow the specific directions for the particular chemical which you intend to use and allow at least 30 minutes for the tablets or drops to take effect. Shake or stir the water several times during the waiting period. If you are using liquid iodine, remember that it is two percent of the strength of the iodine tables and you will need three drops of tincture of iodine per quart. If you use some lemon juice in water that has been purified with helazone tables it will do away with the poor flavor. Also if you shake the water full of bubbles or pour it back and forth to restore the oxygen you will remove the flat taste. You can strain the water if it is extremely dirty before boiling by pouring it through a clean cloth or handkerchief. Other methods of filtering include pouring the water through a bag of sand and then boiling it for 30 minutes, or putting three or four pieces of charcoal from the campfire into a pot of water and boiling it for thirty minutes before using a cloth as a strainer.

WEATHER CONDITIONS

Before you attempt a winter excursion it would be wise

to first master all of the backpacking principles mentioned in this book, in **moderate weather conditions**. Cold temperatures and icy weather are very dangerous, unless you are well prepared, skilled, and knowledgeable concerning winter camping techniques. For below-zero climates, an arctic sleeping (or a nesting bag inside your down one) an expedition style tent, and warm wool clothing is often required in addition to lots of extra padding and large menus of meat-filled meals. Always stay on designated trails that have been maintained for winter hiking, and be wary of avalanche and rock slide dangers, and slick paths. The white world of winter is very beautiful, but demands experience and excellence in the backpacker who would enjoy its charms.

8 The Backpacker's Dream

While you're sitting around home on a blustery, wintery day, part of the joy of backpacking is to dream a little and plan future trips and to look through the suppliers advertising in good outdoor magazines. There are many books, organizations, and agencies that will help the backpacker. Across America is over 15 million acres of wilderness and President Carter is proposing more be added.

Every backpacker has a certain amount of curiosity as to what is over the hill or around the next bend in the trail. There is something about getting away from your roots. At home you were somebody in particular identified with a job, neighborhood, perhaps with a social class, but in backpacking you are on your own. You've chosen to be in that place at that time. Backpacking is a way of seeing America as it was 200 years ago. Areas where only trails exist, where no motor vehicles are allowed, where the earth and its community of life are untraveled by man. Backpacking gives you a chance to search for the place where the crowds aren't; you can meander the hills, cross the wooded ridges that the trails have missed, guided only by your whims and your maps. Only the highest meadows and the farthest far away valleys allude you. There are no bounds. The alpine meadow and the solitary ridge await you. You need neither signpost or trail guide. Backpacking gives you a chance to extend your freedom, to come to respect the land that is part of you. You can travel to the farthest valley or the highest river without fear. It is then that you understand real peace and no matter how men would reach out for you, you're beyond their grasp. And yet, when you return to walk among them, you leave the mountains and meadows behind but you can take with you their strength.

A CROSS COUNTRY LOOK

The great state of California has more wilderness than any other state. In southern California, San Jacinto wilderness is unusual in many ways. It is divided into two sections separated by San Jacinto State Park. The northern portion is wild and rugged and the southern portion is fairly easy going. In northern California, South Warner Wilderness is a favorite of backpacking enthusiasts with a fifteen mile trail at the 9,000 foot level. For other California areas, write: Forest Service, 630 Sanson Street, San Francisco, CA 94104.

Washington and Oregon share over fifteen designated areas; almost all of the high country grandeur of the Northwest. Kalmiopsis in Oregon is one of the low level exceptions and it is unique for its botanical rarities. Washington's Pasayten Wilderness is a virtually unbroken expanse of forty by twenty miles. Meadows, lakes, peaks, just about every wilderness experience is available. For information on more wild lands of the Northwest, write to Forest Service, P.O. 3623, Portland, Oregon 97208.

Montana and Idaho have some of the largest areas devoted to back country preservation. Over a million acres in size, the Sellway-Bitter Root wilderness is the largest in the United States. It is rich in Indian history, solitude, and an immensity of spectacular scenery. The Salmon River drainage and the Salmon River wilderness is unique for backpacking, for nature lovers, and lovers of wild animals. Montana has unexplored areas of mountain wilderness. It was named for the peace that seemed to bear the passage of Lewis and Clark on their historic trek to the Pacific. For more information for these two states, write to Forest Service, Federal Building, Missoula, Montana 59801, or Forest Service Building, Ogden, Utah 84401.

Wyoming offers a string of wilderness in its incredible northwestern corner. Adjacent to the Tetons and to Yellowstone Park are the vast wilds of the summer ranges of the big game and the roots of the mountain men.

The Rocky Mountains of Colorado hold some of the most interesting of all lands for hill walkers and mountaineers. The Maroon Bells-Snow Mass wilderness — "the Bells" — is both accessible and difficult depending upon the choice of route. Good for family backpackers especially because there is a famous hot spring in the south portion. For more information write Forest Service, Denver Federal Center, Denver, Colorado 80225.

New Mexico and Arizona are regions by themselves with wilderness experience from the desert of the Superstitions to the mountains of Winter Peak, smallest wilderness in the West. True desert rats, rockhounds, history buffs, will find treasures in Chiricahua-Gila and San Pedro Parks Wildernesses. These areas are especially attractive in the early spring — March and April. For information on the great Southwest, write Forest Service, Federal Building, Albuquerque, New Mexico 87101.

Unfortunately, due to population development there are very few declared wilderness areas east of the Rocky Mountains. The only lake land wilderness is the boundary waters canoe area in the Superior National Forest in Minnesota. It contains more than a thousand lakes with trails and other routes. Write: Forest Service, 633 W. Wisconsin Ave., Milwaukee, Wisconsin 53203.

In the Southeast, there are two national forest wildernesses. Both of them are in North Carolina and both in the Pisgah National Forest. Lenville Gorge encompasses a twelve mile stretch of the Lenville River. It has many steep slopes, lifts, dropping 2,000 feet. Shining Rock Wilderness has waterfalls, unique geological formations and many trails and springs. For more information, write Forest Service, Suite 800, 1720 Peachtree Road, N.W., Atlanta, Georgia 30309.

The small Great Gulf is the only wilderness area administered by the Forest Service in the Northeast. It encompasses 5,552 acres. It has the lush growth of eastern conifer and hardwood and reaches 5,800 feet at Mt. Washington. It is a wild and remote area. For more information, write Forest Service, 6816 Market, Upper Darby, Pennsylvania 19082.

At the present time only two trails are part of the National Scenic Trail System. The Appalachain Trail goes from Maine to Georgia passing through fourteen states and has many sheltered campsites. The Pacific Crest Trail is rougher. It leads from the desert of the California-Mexico border up the entire length of the Sierra through Oregon and Washington to Canada. For more information on the Appalachian Trail, write to the Appalachian Trail Conference, P.O. Box 236 Wheeling, West Virginia, 25425. The Pacific Crest Club is at P.O. Box 1907, Santa Ana, California 98702.

Through the encouragement of President Carter, other wildernesses are being studied for addition to the Protection of the Wilderness Act. They will not only be in national forests but in national parks and on wildlife refuges as well.

SOURCES OF INFORMATION

You may wish to write to any of the following outfitters for their dream books. Each of them offer a free catalog for you to sit and dream about equipment and supplies that will fill your needs on that dream trip.

1. Abercrombie and Fitch, Madison Avenue at 45, New York, NY 10017

2. L.L. Bean, 278 Main Street, Freeport, ME 04032.

3. Eddie Bower Outfitters, 417 E. Pine St., Seattle, WA 98122.

4. Jerry Mountain Sports, 228 Grant Street, San Francisco, CA 95104.

5. Kelte Pack Inc., P.O. Box 3453, Glendale, CA 92101.

6. Kline Sporting Goods, 227 W. Washington, Chicago, IL 60606

7. Recreation Equipment Inc., 1525 11th Ave., Seattle, WA 918130

8. Wolfe's Sporting Goods, 1200 South State St., Orem, UT 84057

Sources of Trails Information

Heritage Conservation and Recreation Service
Regional Offices

Northwest Region, Federal Building, Room 990, 915 Second Avenue, Seattle, Washington 98174

Pacific Southwest Region, 450 Golden Gate Avenue, San Francisco, California 94102

Mid-Continent Region, Denver Federal Center, P.O. Box 25387, Denver, Colorado 80225

Lake Central Region, Federal Building, Ann Arbor, Michigan 48107

Southeast Region, Richard B. Russell Federal Building, 75 Spring Street, N.W., Atlanta, Georgia 30303

Northeast Region, William J. Green Federal Office Building, Room 9310, 600 Arch Street, Philadelphia, Pennsylvania 19106

South Central Region, 5000 Marble, N.E., Room 211, Albuquerque, New Mexico 87110

Alaska Area Office, 1011 E. Tudor, Suite 297, Anchorage, Alaska 99503

Information concerning the National Scenic and National Historic Trails in the National Trails System can be obtained from the following sources:

Appalachian National Scenic Trail

Appalachian Trail Conference, P.O. Box 236, Harpers Ferry, West Virginia 25425

Appalachian Trail Project Office, National Park Service, P.O. Box 236, Harpers Ferry, West Virginia 25425

Appalachian Mountain Club, 5 Joy Street, Boston, Massachusetts 02108

Potomac Appalachian Trail Club, 1718 N Street, N.W., Washington, D.C. 20036

Pacific Crest National Scenic Trail

Pacific Northwest Regional Office, Forest Service, 319 SW Pine Street, Portland, Oregon 97208

Pacific Crest Club, P.O. Box 1907, Santa Ana, California 92702

California Regional Office, Forest Service, 630 Sansome Street, San Francisco, California 94111

Pacific Crest Foundation, Box 115, Mill City, Oregon 97360

Continental Divide National Scenic Trail

Northern Regional Office, Forest Service, Federal Building, Missoula, Montana 59801

Rocky Mountain Regional Office, Forest Service, 11177 W. 8th Avenue, Box 25127, Lakewood, Colorado 80225

Southwestern Regional Office, Forest Service, 517 Gold Avenue, SW, Albuquerque, New Mexico 87102

Iditarod National Historic Trail

Anchorage District, Bureau of Land Management, 4700 East 72nd Avenue, Anchorage, Alaska 99507

Oregon National Historic Trail

Pacific Northwest Regional Office, National Park Service, Room 931, 4th and Pike Building, 1424 Fourth Avenue, Seattle, Washington 98101

Lewis and Clark National Historic Trail

Midwest Regional Office, National Park Service, 1709 Jackson Street, Omaha, Nebraska 68102

Lewis and Clark Trail Heritage Foundation, Inc., 1097 Chandler Road, Lake Oswego, Oregon 97034

Mormon Pioneer National Historic Trail

Rocky Mountain Regional Office, National Park Service, P.O. Box 25287, Denver, Colorado 80225

Federal Land Managing Agencies

For information about trails in national forests, contact the appropriate Forest Service regional office:

Northern, Federal Building, Missoula, Montana 59801

Rocky Mountain, 11177 W. 8th Ave., Box 25127, Lakewood, Colorado 80225

Southwestern, 517 Gold Avenue SW., Albuquerque, New Mexico 87102

Intermountain, 324 25th Street, Odgen, Utah 84401

California, 630 Sansome Street, San Francisco, California 94111

Pacific Northwest, 319 SW Pine Street, PO Box 3623, Portland, Oregon 97208

Southern, 1720 Peachtree Road NW., Atlanta, Georgia 30309

Eastern, 633 West Wisconsin Avenue, Milwaukee, Wisconsin 53203

Alaska, Federal Office Building, PO Box 1628, Juneau, Alaska 99801

For information about trails in national parks, contact the appropriate regional office of the National Park Service:

North Atlantic Regional Office, National Park Service, 15 State Street, Boston, MA 02109. Phone: (617) 223-2296

National Capital Regional Office, National Park Service, 1100 Ohio Drive, S.W., Washington, D.C. 20242. Phone: (202) 426-6700

Rocky Mountain Regional Office, National Park Service, P.O. Box 25287, Denver, CO 80225. Phone: (303) 234-3095

Southwest Regional Office, National Park Service, Old Sante Fe Trail, P.O. Box 728, Sante Fe, NM 87501. Phone: (505) 988-6375

Pacific Northwest Regional Office, National Park Service, Rm. 931, 4th and Pike Bldg., 1424 Fourth Avenue, Seattle, WA 98101. Phone: (206) 442-7502

Mid-Atlantic Regional Office, National Park Service, 143 South Third Street, Philadelphia, PA 19106, Phone: (215) 597-4367

Midwest Regional Office, National Park Service, 1709 Jackson Street, Omaha, NB 68102. Phone: (402) 221-3471

Southeast Regional Office, National Park Service, Federal Bldg., 75 Spring Street, N.W., Atlanta, GA 30303. Phone: (404) 221-4998

Western Regional Office, National Park Service, 450 Golden Gate Avenue, Box 36063, San Francisco, CA 94102. Phone: (415) 556-4122

Alaska Area Office, National Park Service, 540 West 5th Avenue, Room 202, Anchorage, Alaska 99501. Phone: (907) 276-8166

For information about trail opportunities on Fish and Wildlife Service lands, contact the appropriate Fish and Wildlife Service regional office:

Regional Director, Region 1, Fish and Wildlife Service, Lloyd 500 Building, Suite 1692, 500 N.E. Multnomah Street, Portland, Oregon 97208. Phone: (503) 231-6136

Regional Director, Region 2, Fish and Wildlife Service, U.S. Post Office & Court House, 500 Gold Avenue, S.W., Albuquerque, New Mexico 87103. Phone: (505) 766-2081

Regional Director, Region 3, Fish and Wildlife Service, Federal Bldg., Fort Snelling, Twin Cities, Minnesota 55111. Phone: (612) 725-3585

Regional Director, Region 4, Fish and Wildlife Service, Richard B. Russell Bldg., Suite 1376, 75 Spring Street, S.W., Atlanta, Georgia 30303. Phone (404) 221-6414

Regional Director, Region 5, Fish and Wildlife Service, One Gateway Center, Suite 700, Newton Corner, Massachusetts 02158. Phone: (617) 965-5100

Regional Director, Region 6, Fish and Wildlife Service, P.O. Box 25486, Denver Federal Center, Denver, Colorado 80225. Phone: (303) 234-3865

Alaska Area Office, Fish and Wildlife Service, 1011 East Tudor Road, Anchorage, Alaska 99507. Phone: (907) 276-3800

Director, Fish and Wildlife Service, U.S. Dept. of the Interior, 18th & C Streets, N.W., Washington, D.C. 20240. Phone: (202) 343-7742

State Sources of Trails Information

Northwest Region
Idaho
State Trails Coordinator, Idaho Department of Parks and Recreation, 2177 Warm Springs Avenue, Boise, ID 83720
Oregon
Coordinator, Oregon Recreation Trails System, State Parks Branch, 101 Highway Building, Salem, OR 97310

Washington
State Trails Coordinator, Washington State Interagency, Committee for Outdoor Recreation, 4800 Capitol Boulevard, Tumwater, WA 98504

Pacific Southwest Region
Arizona
Planning Officer, Arizona Outdoor Recreation, Coordinating Commission, 4433 N. 19th Avenue, Suite 203, Phoenix, AZ 85015
Arizona Hiking and Equestrian Trails Committee, Arizona State Parks Board, 1688 West Adams, Phoenix, AZ 85007
California
California Recreational Trails Committee, P.O. Box 2390, Sacramento, CA 95811
Hawaii
Hawaii Department of Land and Natural Resources, P.O. Box 621, Honolulu, HI 96509
Nevada
Administrator, Division of State Parks, 1923 N. Carson Street, Suite 210 Carson City, NV 89710

South Central Region
Arkansas
Park Planner, Arkansas Department of State Parks, One Capitol Mall, Little Rock, AR 72201
Louisiana
Trails Coordinator, Louisiana Office of Program Development, P.O. Box 44247, Baton Rouge, LA 70804
New Mexico
State Parks and Recreation Division, New Mexico Department of Natural Resources, 141 East DeVargas, Santa Fe, NM 87503
Oklahoma
Planner, Division of State Parks, Oklahoma Tourism and Recreation Department, 4020 N. Lincoln, Oklahoma City, OK 73105
Texas
Resource Planner, Comprehensive Planning Branch, Texas Parks and Wildlife Department, 4200 Smith School Road, Austin, TX 78744

Mid-Continent Region

Colorado
Division of Parks and Outdoor Recreation, 1313 Sherman Street, Room 618, Denver, CO 80203

Iowa
Iowa Conservation Commission, 300 Fourth Street, Des Moines, IO 50319

Kansas
Kansas Park and Resources Authority, 503 Kansas Avenue, P.O. Box 977, Topeka, KS 66601

Missouri
Department of Natural Resources, 1203 Jefferson Building, Box 176, Jefferson City, MO 65101

Montana
Recreation and Parks Division, Montana Department of Fish and Game, Mitchell Building, 1420 E. 6th Avenue, Helena, MT 59601

Nebraska
Nebraska Game and Parks Commission, 2200 North 33rd Street. Box 30370, Lincoln, NB 68503

North Dakota
Coordinator, State Outdoor Recreation Agency, R.R. 2, P.O. Box 139, Mandan, ND 58554

Utah
Department of Natural Resources, 807 E. South Temple, Suite 101, Salt Lake City, UT 84102

South Dakota
Department of Game, Fish & Parks, State Office Building, No. 1, Pierre, SD 57501

Wyoming
Director, Wyoming Recreation Commission, 604 East 25th Street, Cheyenne, WY 82002

Lake Central Region

Illinois
Director, Department of Conservation, 602 State Office Building, Springfield, IL 62706

Michigan
Trail Coordinator, Department of Natural Resources, P.O. Box 30028, Lansing, MI 48909

Ohio

Director, Department of Natural Resources, Fountain Square, Building D, Columbus, OH 43224

Indiana

Director, Department of Natural Resources, 608 State Office Bldg., Indianapolis, IN 46204

Minnesota

Commissioner, Department of Natural Resources, 301 Centennial Bldg., St. Paul, MN 55155

Wisconsin

Director of Planning, Wisconsin Department of Natural Resources, Box 7921, Madison, WI 53707

Southeast Region

Alabama

Trails Coordinator, Department of Conservation and Natural Resources, Administrative Building, Montgomery, AL 36130

Florida

Planner, Department of Natural Resources, Division of Recreation and Parks, Crown Building, 202 Blount Street, Tallahassee, FL 32304

Georgia

Trails Planner, Department of Natural Resources, Recreation Planning Section, 703B, 270 Washington Street, S.W., Atlanta, GA 30334

Kentucky

Director, Division of Planning and Grants, State Department of Parks, Capitol Plaza Tower, Room 1107, Frankfort, KY 40601

Mississippi

Planner, Bureau of Outdoor Recreation, Mississippi Park Commission, 2304 Riverside Drive, Jackson, MS 39216

North Carolina

Trails Coordinator, Department of Natural Resources and Community Development, P.O. Box 27687, Raleigh, NC 27611

South Carolina

Department of Parks, Recreation, and Tourism, Edgar A. Brown Building, Suite 113, 1205 Pendleton Street, Columbia, SC, 29201

Tennessee
Trails Administrator, Department of Conservation, 2611 West End Avenue, Nashville, TN 37203
Puerto Rico
Administrator, Public Parks and Recreation Administration, P.O. Box 3207, San Juan, PR 00904
Virgin Islands
Chief Planner, Department of Conservation and Cultural Affairs, P.O. Box 599, Charlotte Amalie, St. Thomas, VI 00801

Northeast Region
Connecticut
Parks and Recreation Unit, Department of Environmental Protection, State Office Building, 165 Capitol Avenue, Hartford, CT 06115
District of Columbia
Director, D.C. Recreation Department, 3149 16th Street, N.W. Washington, DC 20010
Maryland
Secretary, Department of Natural Resources, Tawes State Office Building, Annapolis, MD 21401
New Hampshire
Division of Parks, Department of Resources & Economic Development, P.O. Box 856, State House Annex, Concord, NH 03301
New Jersey
Division of Parks and Forestry, Department of Environmental Protection, Labor and Industry Bldg., Box 1390, Trenton, NJ 08625
Delaware
Division of Parks and Recreation, Department of Natural Resources and Environmental Control, The Edward Tatnall Building, Box 1401, Dover, DE 19901
Maine
Bureau of Parks and Recreation, Department of Conservation, State Office Building, Augusta, ME 04330
Massachusetts
Division of Forests and Parks, Department of Natural Resources, State Office Building, 100 Cambridge Street, Boston, MA 02202

New York
Office of Parks and Recreation, Agency Building #1, Empire State Plaza, Albany, NY 12238
Pennsylvania
Division of State Forest Management, Commonwealth of Pennsylvania, Dept. of Environmental Resources, P.O. Box 1467, Harrisburg, PA 17120
Rhode Island
Chief, Division of Parks and Recreation, Department of Natural Resources, 83 Park Street, Providence, RI 02903
Virginia
Commission of Outdoor Recreation, 8th Street Office Building, 803 E. Broad Street, Richmond, VA 23219
Vermont
Chief, Recreation, Department of Forests and Parks Agency of Environmental Conservation, Montpelier, VT 05602
West Virginia
Chief of Parks and Recreation, Department of Natural Resources, 1800 Washington Street, East, Building 3, Room 330, Charleston, WV 25305

Alaska Area Office
Alaska
Director, Alaska Division of Parks, 619 Warehouse Avenue, Suite 210, Anchorage, AK 99501

Private Organizations

National
National Campers and Hikers Association, Inc., 7172 Transit Road, Buffalo, NY 14221, (Camping, Hiking)
*American Youth Hostels, Inc., National Campus, Delaplane, VA 22025, (Camping, Hiking, Backpacking, and Bicycling)
*Boy Scouts of America, P.O. Box 61030, Dallas/Ft. Worth Airport, TX 75261, (Hiking, Camping)
North American Trail Complex, P.O. Box 805, Bloomington, IN 47401
* American Forestry Association, 1319 18th Street, N.W., Washington, D.C. 20036

National Recreation and Park Association, 1601 N. Kent Street, Arlington, VA 22209

*The Nature Conservancy, 1800 N. Kent Street, Suite 800, Arlington, VA 22209

The American Hiking Society, 317 Pennsylvania Avenue, S.E., Washington, D.C. 20003, Write for Trail Information packets for each state.

American Historical Trails, P.O. Box 810, Washington, D.C. 20044

*Wilderness Society, 1901 Pennsylvania Avenue, Washington, D.C. 20006

*International Backpackers Association, Inc. P.O. Box 85, Lincoln Center, ME 04458

National Trails Council, P.O. Box 1042, St. Charles, IL 60174

*National Wildlife Federation, 1412 16th Street, N.W., Washington, D.C. 20036

*Sierra Club, 220 Bush Street, San Francisco, CA 94104

Northwest Region

Pacific Northwest Trail Association, P.O. Box 1048, Seattle, WA 98111

Federation of Western Outdoor Clubs, 4534½ University Way, N.E., Seattle, WA 98105

The Mountaineers, 719 Pike Street, Seattle, WA 98101

Department of Natural Resources, Public Lands Building, Olympia, WA 98504

Trails Club of Oregon, P.O. Box 1243, Portland, OR 97207

Desert Trail Association, P.O. Box 589, Burns, OR 97720

Center for Environmental Understanding, P.O. Box 332, Spokane, WA 99210

Washington Environmental Council, 107 South Main Street, Seattle, WA 98104

Oregon Environmental Council, 2637 S.W. Water Avenue, Portland, OR 97201

Idaho Alpine Club, Box 2885, Idaho Falls, ID 83401

---

*This organization has a number of member units, chapters, or clubs; detailed information is available from the address listed here.

Idaho Environmental Council, P.O. Box 1708, Idaho Falls, ID 83401

Panhandle Planning and Development Council, P.O. Box 1154, 411 Coeur d'Alene Avenue, Coeur d'Alene, ID, 83814

Wilderness Mountaineering, 204 N. 47th Street, Coeur d'Alene, ID 83814

Wilderness Encounters, P.O. Box 3417, Boise, ID 83703

Oregon Wilderness Coalition, P.O. Box 3066, Eugene, OR 97403

President, Idaho Trail Council, Wildland Recreation Management, College of Forestry, Wildlife and Range Sciences, University of Idaho, Moscow, ID 83843

Idaho Outdoor Association, P.O. Box 7255, Boise, ID 83707

Idaho Natural Areas Coordinating Committee, c/o Forest Research Laboratory, University of Idaho, Moscow, ID 83843

North Idaho Trails Association, 3213 N. Government Way, Coeur d'Alene, ID 83814

Pacific Southwest Region

Southern Arizona Hiking Club, P.O. Box 12122, Tucson, AZ 85711

Arizona Historical Society, 949 East Second Street, Tucson, AZ 85719

Southwest Environmental Service, P.O. Box 2231, Tucson, AZ 85702

Pima County Citizens' Trail Access Committee, 1045 E. Elm Road, Tucson, AZ 85719

High Sierra Packers Association, P.O. Box 123, Madera, CA 93637

San Bernardino County Recreation Trails Council, 24410 Alcudia Road, Hinkley, CA 92347

Santa Cruz Mountains Trail Assn., P.O. Box 1141, Los Altos, CA 94022

Outdoors Unlimited, University of California Recreation Department, 1309 Third Avenue, San Francisco, CA 94107

Hiking Hawaii Tours, 1580 Frear Street, Honolulu, HI 96813

Division of State Parks (Oahu), 1151 Punchbowl Street, Honolulu, HI 96813

Division of State Parks (Hawaii), 75 Aupuni Street, Hilo, HI 96720

Santa Barbara Trails Council, 4410 Marina Drive, Santa Barbara, CA 93110

Alpine Guide, P.O. Box 291, Culver City, CA 90230

Northern California Trails Council, Wilderness Road, Branscomb, CA 95417

Regional Trails Coordinator, East Bay Regional Park District, 11500 Skyline Boulevard, Oakland, CA 94619

La Canada-Flintridge Trails Council, Box 852, La Canada, CA 91011

Skyline Regional Trails Council, P.O. Box 1141, Los Altos, CA 94022

San Luis Obispo Trails Council, 8979 Junipero Avenue, Atascadero, CA 93422

Trails West, Inc., 630 Stanford Way, Sparks, NV 89413

Hawaiian Trail and Mountain Club, P.O. Box 2238, Honolulu, HI 96804

Division of State Parks (Kauai), 3060 Elwa Street, Lihue, HI 96766

Division of State Parks (Maui and Molokai), 54 High Street, Wailuku, HI 96793

South Central Region

Executive Secretary, Arkansas Trails Council, c/o Arkansas State Parks, One Capitol Mall, Little Rock, AR 72201

The Backpacker, 3378 Highland Road, Baton Rouge, LA 70802

New Mexico National Recreation and Park Association, 505 Central Avenue, N.W., Albuquerque, NM 87102

President, Ozark Society, c/o Arkansas Highway Department, P.O. Box 2261, Little Rock, AR 72203

Ozark Society, 2811 East 22nd, Tulsa, OK 74114

Chairman of Trails, 12315 Ann Lane, Houston, TX 77040

Mid-Continent Region

Colorado Mountain Club, 2530 W. Alameda, Denver, CO 80219

Colorado Mountain Trails Foundation, P.O. Box 15427, Denver, CO 80215

American Camping Association, Rocky Mountain Section, 6928 S. Broadway, Littleton, CO 80122

Kansas Trails Council, Box 3162, Shawnee Mission, KS 66203

Wyoming Outdoor Council, Inc., 202½ S. Second, Laramie, WY 82070

Wasatch Mountain Club, 3155 Highline Drive, Salt Lake City, UT 84106

Wyoming Mountain Men Trails Foundation, Route 1, Box 75, Cheyenne, WY 82001

Montana Wildlife Federation, 410 Woodworth Avenue, Missoula, MT 59801

Utah Trails Council, Weber County Planning Commission, Municipal Building, Room 714, Ogden, UT 84401

Lake Central Region

Executive Director, Michigan United Conservation Clubs, Inc., Box 2235, Lansing, MI 48911

Bikeway Council Coordinator, Illinois Department of Transportation, 2300 South Dirksen Parkway, Springfield, IL 62704

State Hiking Director, National Campers and Hikers Assn., 319 W. Cass, Greenville, MI 48838

Indiana Division of Tourism, Department of Commerce, 336 State House, Indianapolis, IN 46204

Forestry Agent, University of Wisconsin Extension, Box 460, Antigo, WI 54409

Buckeye Trail Association, Inc., P.O. Box 254, Worthington, OH 43085

Ice Age Park and Trail Foundation of Wisconsin, Inc., 780 North Water Street, Milwaukee, WI 53202

The Illinois Prairie Path, 616 Delles Road, Wheaton, IL 60187

Southeast Region

Alabama Trails Association, 938 So. 80th Street, Birmingham, AL 35206

Bartram Trail Conference, 3815 Interstate Court, Suite 202, Montgomery, AL 36109

Vulcan Trail Association, 4609 7th Court South, Birmingham, AL 35222

Florida Trail Association, Inc., 4410 N.W. 18th Place, Gainesville, FL 32604

Georgia Appalachian Trail Club, Box 654, Atlanta, GA 30301

Kentucky Trails Association, P.O. Box 784, Louisville, KY 40201

Carolina Mountain Club, 17 Darcey Lane, Asheville, NC 28805

Natahala Hiking Club, Route 3, Box 131, Sylva, NC 28779

Tennessee Trails Association, P.O. Box 4913, Chattanooga, TN 37405

Smokey Mountain Hike Club, Route 3, Antioch Ch. Road, Lenoir City, TN 37771

Northeast Region

Connecticut Forest and Park Association, Inc., 1010 Main Street, P.O. Box 389, East Hartford, CT 06108

Potomac Appalachian Trail Club, 1718 N Street, N.W., Washington, D.C. 20036

*International Backpackers Asso., Inc., P.O. Box 85, Lincoln Center, ME 04458

Mountain Club of Maryland, 14 Solar Circle, Baltimore, MD 21234

*Appalachian Mountain Club, 5 Joy Street, Boston, MA 02108

1/*New England Trails Conference, 33 Knollwood Drive, East Longmeadow, MA 01028

*New York-New Jersey Trail Conference, 15 East 40th Street, New York, NY 10016

*Adirondack Mountain Club, Inc., 172 Ridge Street, Glens Falls, NY 12801

*Finger Lakes Trails Conference, Box 18040, Rochester, NY 14618

*Keystone Trail Association, RD 3, Box 261, Cogan Station, PA 17728

Green Mountain Club, Box 54, Rutland, VT 05701 (Long Trail in Vermont)

*Virginia Trails Association, 13 West Maple Street, Alexandria, VA 22301

West Virginia Scenic Trails Association, P.O. Box 4042, Charleston, W.Va. 25304

*Appalachian Trail Conference, Inc., P.O. Box 236, Harpers Ferry, W.Va. 25425

Alaska Area Office

Alaska Wildlife Federation and Sportsmen's Council, Inc., Box 3072, Route 3, Juneau, AK 99801

Mountaineering Club of Alaska, Box 2037, Anchorage, AK 99510

Iditarod Trail Committee, Knik Road, Box 5460, Wasilla, AK 99687

Alaska Alpine Club, c/o John Davies, Geophysical Institute, University of Alaska, P.O. Box 81-200, Fairbanks, AK 99701

Alaska Travel Division, Pouch E, Juneau, AK 99801

Southeast Alaska Mountaineering Club, c/o Ed Brown, Box 895, Ward Cove, AK 99928

1/ address changes with annual election of officers.   Current address available from the Appalachian Trail Conference, Inc.

*Organization has a number of member units, chapters, or clubs. Additional information is available from the address listed here.

Notes